I'm Praying for you

A Collection of Life Giving Prayers

Dr. Karren D. Todd

Dr. Karren D. Todd

I'm Praying for You
A Collection of Life Giving Prayers

by Dr. Karren D. Todd
ISBN 978-1-7322339-1-1

Copyright © 2020 Karren Todd
Memphis, TN

All rights reserved. No part of this book may be reproduced in a form or by any means without the prior written consent of the publisher, excepting brief quotes used in reviews.

First printing: December 2020.
10 9 8 7 6 5 4 3 2 1

Cover design by JoVenTosh.
Interior design by Suzan David.

Printed in the United States of America.
Unless otherwise indicated, Scripture references are from the New International Version.

Other Books by Dr. Todd
    Believe: God Can. God Will.
    One is a Whole Number: Recovering The Joy of Being Single
    Power Walk: 40 Day Journey to Power

Dedication

This book is dedicated to my big little brother Bobby Todd, Jr. who entered into eternal rest in the middle of this process. Bobby worked nights so he was usually awake when I made every early morning post.

One of his last posts was August 27, 2020. It said:
"Up early to catch the morning inspiration Karren Todd."

I miss him dearly but I am grateful that God used me to inspire him while he was on this side of heaven.

Dr. Karren D. Todd

Acknowledgements

Thank you to all of my social media friends who check in daily for a word of prayer and literally demanded this collection. This has been my assignment for the past 9 months and it has been my pleasure. I don't know if there is an end date to posting prayers on social media but there will never be an end date for praying

Thank you Alicia Hill and Regina Butts for scrolling through months of posts and compiling over 250 prayers! Jo'V ~ your photography and graphic design skills are unmatched. Thank you Sherronda Johnson for keeping me on task and pulling this collection of love together. You are alright with me!

I'm Praying For You

Contents

Dedication	D
Acknowledgements	E
Daily Prayers	1
Weekly Prayers	71
Prayers for Self-Care	85
Healing Scriptures	93
Names of God	101
Hebrew Names of God	102
Other Names Ascribed To God Throughout Scripture	106
Dr. Karren D. Todd	108

Dr. Karren D. Todd

Daily Prayers

Rejoice in hope, be patient in tribulation, be constant in prayer. (Romans 12:12 ESV)

As you pray these prayers, my hope is that you are able to rejoice in hope, be patient in troubled times and consistently seek God for everything. I pray these daily prayers can assist you in building a habit of praying for yourself and for others.

Each prayer is titled "Today's Prayer." No dates. No sequential order. Whichever prayer you read or whichever prayer you need - that is your prayer for today.

Through prayer, may your faith be increased, your joy be abundant, and your purpose be fulfilled.

I love you and I'm praying for you.

~ Karren

Today's Prayer

I am praying for God to help settle your mind. There is only so much you can process and still make sound decisions. Your mind is racing. Your thoughts are all over the place. Balls are dropping because you can't stay focused long enough to finish your thoughts ~ let alone finish the actual projects that you are thinking about.

It's time to make some tough decisions and take some of these mentally draining things off your plate. I know it's hard and you think everything you are doing is equally important ~ it's not. You just don't want to disappoint the person that you overcommitted to. Even if you have become used to the dysfunction of being pulled in many directions at once ~ this is NOT the season for that. I pray that God will give you the courage to say NO today.

As you align with God, I speak divine peace to overtake you. I bind stressful, wayward thoughts and release a spiritual calmness that centers you and allows you to keep your mind on the things that matter. I speak that you will have the audacity to turn down invitations and people that don't serve God's purpose for you in this season. I pray that you will be brave enough to guard your sacred space and in return you will experience the harmony of your mind, body and spirit that you have been missing. Take a deep breath. Make the decision.

It's going to be so worth it. I'm praying for you.

Today's Prayer

I will trust God. I will not worry about what I cannot control.
I will trust God. I will work daily and diligently to replace anxiety with peace.
I will trust God. I will operate in faith AND I will do the work.
I will trust God. With every breath, every decision, every step.
I will trust God. For my provision, my protection and my purpose.
I will trust God.

Today's Prayer

This is the day that the Lord has made. Let us rejoice and be glad in it! I pray, today, that God will remind you of the reasons you have to rejoice. It is so easy in this time of fear and anxiety to rewind our mental movies of pain, grief and heartache.

Today I pray you would shift your thoughts to the goodness of God. God has been good to you! With sickness all around, Jehovah Rophe has kept you. In the valley of the shadow of death, Jehovah Rohi has been your guide. Even in times of isolation and loneliness, Jehovah Shammah has been the Ever Present One. God is a good God and God's mercy endures forever!

I decree and declare God's peace in your spirit today. I speak that as you rejoice, God will break the strongholds of fear and increase your faith based on His track record in your life. According to God's word, I speak a peace that will guard your heart and your mind as you release your anxieties in the presence of Jehovah Shalom. For this is the day that the Lord has made, we will rejoice and we will be glad in it! I love you and I'm praying for you.

*Jehovah Rophe: The Lord My Healer
*Jehovah Rohi: The Lord My Shepherd
*Jehovah Shammah: The Lord is There
*Jehovah Shalom: The Lord of Our Peace

Today's Prayer

God, I pray that you would grant us clarity and heightened discernment in times of trouble. I pray that in all the noise and with all of the distractions, that we will be able to hear your voice above a whisper. I speak that we will be wise as serpents and innocent (harmless) as doves. I pray that we would use divine wisdom in our decision making and that those decisions would not bring harm to us, to those around us, and neither will they harm the future you have laid out for us. Guide us, O thou great Jehovah, as we pilgrim through this barren land. We are weak, but thou art mighty. Hold us with your powerful hand.

I offer this prayer in Jesus' name, Amen.

Today's Prayer

Thank you, God, for being my joy and my strength. I bless You because You remove my pain, misery and strife. Thank You for Your promises, O God! Thank You for promising to keep me and never leave me ~ I know that You won't go back on Your word.

Now God, help me to fast and pray and stay on the path that You have designed for me. Help me to keep my life, my words and my actions clean and clear from the habits that pull my attention from You.

My desire is to be in Your will. My desire is to be with You for eternity. I've worked too hard and come too far from who I used to be and what I used to do and how I used to think. I will NOT turn back! You are my all and all. I love You. I honor You. I bless Your Holy Name!

In Jesus' name, I pray and give thanks. Hallelujah and Amen.

Today's Prayer

This morning I heard: *On your mark. Get Set. Go!* I got excited about GO...then I heard: *"but are you on YOUR mark?"* We are all ready to run to the next blessing but we don't want to start from our mark. There is work to be done. GO is near. Get on your mark.

God help us to get ON THE MARK that is aligned with our destiny. Our desire is to RUN to Your promise but we are realizing that running just anywhere won't get us to divine purpose. There is a path to our purpose. So, God, I speak that you will lead us, guide us, push us, pull us, lift us up, snatch us back, move us over and love us through.

We surrender! DIRECT us now God ~ so that You won't have to DETOUR us later. God, I speak that this week will be productive for the one who is reading this right now. I speak an abundance of peace, a divine dispensation of God's favor and a release of creativity that produces an increase in finances in the name of Jesus. God, we won't just name and claim the blessing. We will do our part and get on the mark. This way we can be SET when God says GO! I pray this prayer in the name of the One who got on HIS mark, followed His path to the Cross and fulfilled God's Plan so that we could receive God's Promise.

In Jesus' name. Amen.

Today's Prayer

The POWER is in the WORD. READ it until you UNDERSTAND it so that you can LIVE it.

Proverbs 3-5

Trust in the Lord with all your heart and lean not on your own understanding; in all your ways submit to God, and God will make your paths straight. Do not be wise in your own eyes; fear the Lord and shun evil. This will bring health to your body and nourishment to your bones. (NIV)

Trust in the Lord with all your heart; do not depend on your own understanding. Seek God's will in all you do, and God will show you which path to take. Don't be impressed with your own wisdom. Instead, fear the Lord and turn away from evil. Then you will have healing for your body and strength for your bones. (NLT)

Trust God from the bottom of your heart; don't try to figure out everything on your own. Listen for God's voice in everything you do, everywhere you go; God is the one who will keep you on track. Don't assume that you know it all. Run to God! Run from evil! Your body will glow with health, your very bones will vibrate with life! (MSG)

Today's Prayer

I know that times may be hard right now. I know that your faith may be challenged right now. I know that with all that you have prayed for ~ doubt may be creeping in right now.

Yet I pray that doubt has not changed what you KNOW about God.

God WILL make a way. God WILL fight for you.

God WILL hear and answer your prayers. God IS on the way!

I WILL bless the Lord at all times and God's praises shall continually be in my mouth!

ALL times include "uncertain times!" So now every time I hear this phrase, I will be reminded that THIS is a time to BLESS THE LORD!

I am praising with you and I am praying for you.

Today's Prayer

I pray you hear God speak and see God move ALL day today. Slow down. Pay attention. Trust your connection. I pray that when you hear the WORD that's for you, you will experience an overwhelming moment of PEACE. I pray that when that divine calmness settles your spirit, relieves your anxiety and dispels your fear ~ you will KNOW that you have had a moment with God. Have an amazing day!

I'm praying for you.

Today's Prayer

Praying for the ones who know what you could be doing/producing/creating/experiencing, but it seems like something is keeping you stuck or stagnant. It seems like every time you get close to your purpose or close to God's promise or even close to your peace ~ something else comes to attack or distract you. I pray that the Holy Spirit will mind the gap for you right now, in the name of Jesus.

I intercede in prayer on your behalf. I bind every plot, plan, scheme, trick and strategy of the enemy. In the name and authority of Jesus Christ and by the power of His shed blood, I command the enemy to loose his hold on your hope, loose his hold on your peace, loose his hold on your finances. Any demonic presence that has attempted to attach itself to you is rendered powerless and ineffective. Tormenting spirits are cast out never to return. I speak that the assignment is over. I speak that the assignment is over. I speak that the assignment is over! Release the one reading this right now, in the name of Jesus, and return to hell empty-handed! Strongholds are broken. Yokes are destroyed. According to God's word, I loose peace and protection right now in the name of Jesus. And it IS so!

Hallelujah and Amen!

Today's Prayer

This morning I speak a Deuteronomy 28 blessing over your life. I speak that you will be blessed in the city and in the field. You will be blessed when you come in and blessed when you go out. Those that come against you will be defeated in the name of Jesus! I pray that God will bless your home and all that you put your hands to.

As you walk in obedience, God will establish you and grant you abundant prosperity. I decree according to God's word that you will live under an open heaven. You will be ahead in your business endeavors and never behind. You will be the lender (of money and ideas) and never the borrower. You will be above the standard and never beneath. I speak this for your home and for your business.

God is about to send opportunities your way that you never thought you would be a part of. It will seem TOO big. It's not. You serve a BIG GOD that releases BIG things to create BIG futures for those who love Him. Be blessed, my friend.

I'm praying for you.

Today's Prayer

If this is for you, I pray you "hear it" as truth in love. Pay attention today. Stop looking at everything on the surface. There are things happening that mean more than they seem. There are things being said that have a deeper meaning. You're missing divine instructions and ignoring red flags because you're taking everything at face value. You'll save yourself some time and unnecessary heartache if you would just slow down. LISTEN to what you hear and PROCESS what you see.

God is showing you YOUR answer and giving you YOUR solution. Stop saying God ain't speaking when you ain't listening. Check your emotions. You're too mad, or too disappointed, or too bitter, or too in love to see what God is showing you. I'm praying for your clarity ~ to see and hear with divine focus. I speak discernment to trust what you feel in your gut and an increase in courage to take action based on God's instruction. NOW... slow down and read this again. I'm praying that it hits the spirit of whoever needs it.

I'm always praying for you.

Today's Prayer

Praying for every person who is working toward a dream. Whether you are working on your own business, working to climb the corporate ladder, or working to do both. I'm praying for you. I speak that whatever you do, you will work for God and not for man ~ knowing that it is from the Lord that you will receive your reward.

I decree according to God's word that as you commit your work to the Lord- your plans will be established. I declare the favor of the Lord our God be upon you and establish the work of your hands. I speak that God will do exceedingly and abundantly more than you can ask, think or dare to imagine according to God's power that is inside you. God's power will enable you. God's power will strengthen you.

I bind being on pins and needles about what the government will decide concerning your finances. I pray for a release of God's "Cares Act". I pray that God will open the windows of heaven and pour out God's stimulus and we won't have room enough to receive it! Nothing is impossible with God. Nothing is impossible with God. Nothing is impossible with God!

You serve a BIG GOD who allows you to dream BIG. You serve the Creator of the ENTIRE universe. God spoke it and it was. AND it was GOOD! I pray that God will just start dropping ideas for products, for marketing and for branding TODAY in the name of Jesus!

I speak divine creativity in your area of work. I speak the promise of God that you will eat the fruit of the labor of your hands. You will be blessed and it will be well with you. New clients and customers. It is so! New sponsors. New donors. It is so! New products. New niches. It is so! New markets. New regions. New suppliers. It is so in the name of Jesus! I believe that God is able! I'll pray for you. You pray for me. We'll watch God change things.

Hallelujah and Amen.

Today's Prayer

I'm studying Elijah and I kept hearing: *God is about to speak.* In I Kings 17, God is caring for Elijah during a drought. Ravens are bringing him food and he is drinking from a brook. (A whole "nother" sermon for another day.)

⁷Some time later the brook dried up because there had been no rain in the land. ⁸ Then the word of the Lord came to him: (I Kings 17:7-8 NIV)

First, the brook dried up THEN God spoke. *Read that again.* Now, it took time for the brook to dry up, which means Elijah watched it happen. I can imagine the fear and anxiety that came as the supply got smaller and smaller. You are watching things dry up in your life. Opportunities drying up. Investments and savings drying up. Relationships drying up. But the good news is GOD IS ABOUT TO SPEAK!

God is about to send a word for your provision. God is about to show you the way that God has already made. God is about to direct you to the door that God has already opened. I pray that you don't get so anxious about not having enough that you can't hear God directing you to your provision. It's getting real uncomfortable. Resources are drying up. But hold on...the SOURCE is about to speak!!

I'm praying for you.

Today's Prayer

Trust God in this place. You have been waiting on God to open a door of opportunity in front of you. Make sure you have closed the doors that are behind you. You've got too many loose ends and "just in case" doors open. Let go of some of your fall back options (and fall back people) and trust God COMPLETELY.

Commit your way to the Lord; trust also in Him and He shall bring it to pass. (Psalm 37:5 NKJV)

God, help me to commit my plans to you; knowing that your ways are higher than my ways and your thoughts are higher than my thoughts. Help me to trust You MORE. I believe that you are able to make it happen. Help me to believe that You will make it happen for me. I want to trust you COMPLETELY. Help me to see what doors I need to close so that You can open the doors that lead to my destiny.

Today's Prayer

God, we plead the blood of Jesus over every frontline healthcare worker. Loose your angels to protect them from all hurt, harm and danger as they go into battle every day. Increase their wisdom and discernment as they care for those who cannot care for themselves. We bind all mishaps and freak accidents that could expose them. We cancel every plot, plan, scheme, or trick of the enemy to use their anxiety or their exhaustion against them. Be their covering, O God! Cover their minds, cover their health, cover their families, cover their finances and cover their bodies as they risk their lives fighting for the lives of others.

God, release Your favor, Your anointing and Your peace that goes beyond our understanding. You are Jehovah Rohi ~ God Our Shepherd! Be their shepherd, God. Lead them, guide them and keep them safe. We know You can and we believe You will. We offer this prayer in the name of the One who saves and makes safe, the matchless name of Jesus Christ.

Amen.

Today's Prayer

Praying for the ones who were already experiencing trauma and anxiety before the pandemic. The ones who were in the middle of life-changing decisions or who were already dealing with sickness, depression and financial strain. You were already at the end of your rope and now it feels that someone has cut the rope in the middle. I pray that you will not make decisions out of panic and you will not be overcome by seeing the trouble on every side. God, I ask that you would show up in their situation and command a reprieve, in the name of Jesus. You, O God, have the power to solve EVERY problem with ONE word.

Speak, Lord! If it is not in your will to make it ALL go away, I ask that you command a release in one area. Demand relief from one issue. Relieve some of the pressure, God, to let them know that You are fighting for them. That even in this, You are with them. Lord, if you won't stop the storm, please give them peace and strength to anchor them in the middle of it. This is your servant's prayer. In the name of Jesus ~ the One who SAVES!

Amen.

Today's Prayer

Isaiah 33:2

Lord, be gracious to us; we long for you. Be our strength every morning, our salvation in time of distress. (NIV)

God, treat us kindly. You're our only hope. First thing in the morning, be there for us! When things go bad, help us out! (MSG)

Thank you, God, for your grace. Thank you for your love and kindness. Even in this, my hope is still in you. I am so grateful that You are present every morning with strength and new mercy for the new day. I am also grateful that when things don't turn out like I planned ~ even if it's my fault ~ You still show up for me. I know You will show up again and be God. I will wait for You. You will show up and change the situation or You will show up and change ME in the situation. You are my help and MY help is on the way. I will wait for You. I offer this prayer in the name of the One who showed up to save us, Jesus Christ. He did it before. He will do it again.

Hallelujah and Amen.

Today's Prayer

I am a firm believer that God hears and answers prayer. Today, I am praying for the ones who are dealing with God's "NO". The ones who are STILL waiting because God denied the request. I pray that you can allow God to heal your heart: even if it's God's response that caused it to break. I speak that you will stop looking at closed doors and walk toward the one that is open. What you felt as rejection was just REDIRECTION. I pray that you can reconcile your pain with God's power and your sadness with God's Sovereignty. God is a BIG God. God has more. God has better. But you will never get to NEXT staring at NO. Lean NOT to your own understanding. Trust God's plan.

I'm praying for you.

Today's Prayer

God, I thank you for the praise that is bubbling up in my spirit. I thank you for THIS JOY that I have ~ the world didn't give it to me and the world can't take it away. I am forever grateful that the only way I know how to go through is to PRAY through and to PRAISE through. So, I will bless the Lord at all times and His praise shall continually be in my mouth. My soul shall make its boast in the Lord ~ the humble shall hear of it and be glad. Oh, MAGNIFY the Lord with me, and let us exalt His name together!

God, I pray that you will RELEASE an unspeakable, unexplainable and undeniable JOY to my friend who is reading this right now. And we will be careful to give you all the praise, all the glory and all the honor. We pray this in the name of the One who brings the FULLNESS OF JOY ~ Jesus Christ.

Amen and Amen.

Today's Prayer

Praying for those who feel as if they have been thrown in the air with no safe place to land. I speak that God will send God's love to lift you and we will watch you SOAR through this crisis. I speak that you will stay the course of your faith. According to God's Word, I decree a RENEWED STRENGTH in the name of Jesus. Strength to run and not be weary. Strength to walk and not faint. Strength to mount up on wings like eagles and SOAR. I speak it and believe it to be so in the name of One who saves and keeps us safe- His name is Jesus.

And all the believers said, "Amen."

Today's Prayer

Praying for the ones who are considering a life-changing decision. Being in crisis mode has made you reflective of your life choices ~ careers, relationships, church affiliations...everything. Crisis, trauma and/or loss has made you realize just how short life is and your current life is not how you want to live anymore. I pray that God gives you clarity in your thought process. I bind knee jerk reactions and release an Issachar anointing with divine wisdom and revelation for every decision. If this is your season for change, I pray you embrace it.

Walk into it boldly. If God shows you change but instructs you to wait, I pray you wait gracefully and don't jump ahead of God's timing. I pray you trust what you know about God above your anxiousness, so that your next move will be aligned with God's plans and will position you for your destiny.

I'm praying for you.

Today's Prayer

Praying for the ones who anchored their faith to wait out the storm. God says it's time to MOVE in the storm. Even storms produce momentum. I pray that you will MOVE in spite of the external uncertainty because God is birthing a divine certainty inside of you. Listen, God is not obligated to hold your "next" until you are comfortable. You have received several confirmations, but you have not moved. This means you need accountability.

There are people in your circle that you have not shared the move with because they will push you and hold you accountable. Stop dodging accountability. Stop talking about you moving in silence. Bruh, some of y'all silent cause you ain't moving. *(my words not God's)* It's time for you to pick up your mat and WALK. Pick up your plan and ACT. Pick up your faith and MOVE!

I'm praying for you.

Today's Prayer

Thank You, God, for showing up for me. You've shown up in ways that I needed; in ways that I didn't know I needed and even in ways I couldn't imagine. Thank You for making a way! Thank You for easing my pain! Thank You for carrying me through! Thank You for dropping solutions in my spirit. I know that if You did it for me You will do it for my friend that is reading this right now! Do it for her, God! Do it for him, God!

Do it so big and so wide open that everyone around will have to say, "That wasn't nobody but God!" Don't just blow our minds God ~ Blow the minds of the people who are watching and KNOW we believe in You. Let them see how BIG our God is so that they will try You for themselves. Get glory out of our lives in the name of Jesus!

I decree and declare that this week we will PRAY MORE in Your name, we will HEAR MORE from Your word and we will DO MORE in Your will. We stand on tiptoe in anticipation for a move of God this week that is exceedingly abundantly MORE than we can ask or think or dare to imagine. We speak it and it IS so! In the name and authority of the One who can give more than we have room enough to receive.

In Jesus' name ~ Hallelujah and Amen!

Today's Prayer

When Paul was writing to Timothy, he reminded Timothy twice to GUARD THE DEPOSIT that was entrusted to him. Life can pull you away from your foundation. People and past experiences can make you doubt what you KNOW you heard God say. Then one day you will look up and your behaviors and habits and thoughts are a long way from the core of who you really are. *(Just say "ouch" and keep reading)* God has made valuable deposits in you.

Deposits that can change your life and the lives of the people attached to you. God has even deposited things in you that will give hope to people who are watching you ~ but will never say anything to you. By the power of the Holy Spirit, I speak that you will guard the deposit that has been entrusted to you. Guard your faith. Guard your joy. Guard your peace. Guard your dreams. God is trusting you. There is work to be done.

I'm praying for you.

Today's Prayer

Praying for the ones who can help everyone else see their potential and work toward their dreams ~ but they can't seem to do it for themselves. I'm praying for you as you genuinely celebrate the success of others and try to wait patiently on your turn. I'm praying that your frustration with God's timing in your life does not make you question God's purpose for you. You have been disappointed lately and even had thoughts to stop helping others move forward because you haven't moved forward. Those thoughts are not from God.

I speak that the Holy Spirit will begin to push them back in the name of Jesus. I pray that God will send help for the helpers. I pray that God sends you ~ a YOU! Someone to help you strategize, someone to help cheer you on, someone to talk you through the hard parts. You are a GIFT to those around you. Continue to be the light. God is about to reward your faithfulness.

I'm praying for you.

Today's Prayer

You are not defeated. All hope is not gone. It is not time to surrender. I know it is dark right now, but don't give up in the dark what God promised in the light. The little that you have right now is all God needs to work things in your favor. I speak that your mustard seed faith is about to cause the mountain to MOVE! God WILL make a way! God WILL provide! God WILL heal!

According to God's word, I decree and declare strength in your weakness, joy in your sorrow and peace in your storm. Stay rooted in God's Word and grounded in your faith. God is about to give you beauty for ashes.

I'm praying for you.

Today's Prayer

We need to learn to REACH for God. Think of a baby who cries out so that anyone can help. Then imagine a toddler who reaches for the person that she/he KNOWS can help. God is showing me that some of us are just crying out for ANYBODY to help or make us feel better. However, as more mature believers, we need to intentionally reach for the One we KNOW can help. I speak that you will be more intentional in your faith. I decree and declare that as we move through these crises, we will also move from milk to meat in the understanding and application of spiritual disciplines.

I speak that in this season and those to come, we will stretch our arms up through PRAYER, cry out in WORSHIP and stand on our tiptoes through PRAISE. We will reach for the One who can pick us up, care for us and make everything alright. I speak all of this in the name of the One who can work it out for our good.

In Jesus' name. I'm praying for you.

Today's Prayer

Do not take revenge, my dear friends, but leave room for God's wrath, for it is written: "It is mine to avenge; I will repay," says the Lord.
(Romans 12:19 NIV)

The enemy is using anger and shame to grow a spirit of vengeance in the hearts of believers. You ARE praying more, but you have grudges that you won't let go of. I want your prayers to be effective! So listen, I know they did you wrong... however... stop trying to get back at them. Stop trying to embarrass them because they embarrassed you. Stop trying to hurt them because they hurt you.

You are delaying the promises of God in your life. As a result of what YOU are doing, you can't hear God clearly. You can't move forward. Please understand that you STILL have to reap what YOU sow- even if you believe they deserve it. I pray you can release the anger and the shame, the hurt and the pain. I speak forgiveness in your heart, divine power to release them from your thoughts, strength to take your hands out of it and patience to leave room for the justice of God.

It's tight but it's right. I'm praying for you.

Today's Prayer

Praying for the ones who are struggling with their faith. Some have not lost faith completely, but you are fighting to believe the things that you used to be sure about. God has not forgotten about you. God is sending help for the fight. I know it seems really dark. Everything seems heavy. Nothing seems like it's working. I encourage you to keep waking up and keep showing up. God will meet you at the point of your need. God has not forgotten about you.

I bind the spirit of heaviness and declare according to God's word that no harm will overtake you. I bind the spirit of suicide in the name of Jesus. I decree according to God's word that you shall live and not die. Giving up is not going to work because the world still needs you. You are still a part of God's plan. Even when you can't find the words to pray ~ there are others praying for you. I am not the only one.

The Holy Spirit is interceding on your behalf! Whether it's sickness, depression, loneliness or whatever situation is making you feel like you are losing ~ You are NOT fighting alone. Prayer warriors everywhere are praying for you right now! Prayer warriors EVERYWHERE are praying for you right now! And the surge of hope that you felt when you read that is proof that you still have faith! Hold on. God has not forgotten about you.

WE are praying for you.

Today's Prayer

God, according to Your Word, give us strength. Bless us with Your peace as we live through what we cannot control. A strength that allows us to keep pressing... with a peace that surpasses our understanding. This is our prayer in Jesus' name, Amen.

Now pray it again and make it personal. Replace "us" with me, "we" with I, and "our" with my.

Today's Prayer

The Lord will give [unyielding and impenetrable] strength to His people; The Lord will bless His people with peace.

(Psalm 29:11 AMP)

UNYIELDING: not giving way to pressure; unlikely to be swayed.

IMPENETRABLE: impossible to pass through or enter; impossible to understand.

Lord, we thank you for an unyielding strength. For a strength that does not give way to pressure. A strength that does not submit to pressure. For a strength that will not be swayed in the name of Jesus. We bless your name right now for an impenetrable strength. A strength that is impossible for fear to pass through. A strength that is impossible for worry and anxiety to enter. Even impossible for those who do not believe to fully understand.

Thank you, God, for Your divine strength! Now, God, we rest in your Word that says You will bless us with peace. We decree YOUR word and we declare it to be so, in the mighty and matchless name of Jesus.

Amen.

Today's Prayer

The situation you are in isn't punishment. It's PREPARATION. God is TRAINING you. Ironically, you keep praying for God to release you from the very thing that is preparing you for what YOU prayed for! God knows what you need because God knows what's coming.

I pray that you surrender to God's training so that you can handle what's coming. I pray that you change your lens so that you can see the growth that needs to take place. I pray that you change your perspective to realize God corrects because God cares. I pray that you learn the lesson so that you can carry out the next matter in your life.

Remember those times you got excited when the preacher said "Get Ready! Get Ready! Get Ready!" Well, THIS is what "getting ready" looks like. God loves you. God is not just preparing you to GET the blessing. God is preparing you so that you will be able to KEEP the blessing. Change your perspective. Learn the lesson. Keep the blessing.

I'm praying for you.

Today's Prayer

Sometimes life happens and knocks the wind out of us. God, I pray that as I navigate life's circumstances, I will have PEACE as God works things together for my good. I pray God's forgiveness for the things that I did or did not do. I pray God's favor for all the things that God is able to do. I decree according to Your Word and Your Works that even with my MANY imperfections, I STILL meet the qualifications for Your DIVINE INTERVENTION. Move on my behalf in the name of Jesus!

I speak that because of God's grace and my gratefulness, things will happen today for my good that will have God's fingerprints all over them. Miracles will happen. Breakthroughs will happen. Opportunities will happen. I speak it and it is so!

This is my prayer in Jesus' name, Hallelujah and Amen.

Today's Prayer

Morning worship and prayer (based on Psalm 121):

Lord, I will lift my eyes to the hills, Knowing my HELP is coming from You, Your PEACE You give me in times of the storm, You are the SOURCE of my strength, You are the STRENGTH of my life, I lift my hands in total PRAISE to You.

God, I thank you for your HELP. Your help that is keeping me now and Your help that is on the way. God, I thank You for Your PEACE. In the middle of the storms that I am facing, I receive Your peace which is beyond my understanding. God, I bless You for being my SOURCE. I honor You and You alone as I realize that everything else in my life is a resource that my Source has provided just for me.

I thank you right now God for being my STRENGTH. I speak Your strength over my mind during these traumatic times. I speak Your strength over my heart during these heartbreaking times of loss. And I speak Your strength to my body as I receive Your healing from the top of my head to the depths of my soul. Now, God as I surrender to Your Word and to Your Will, I lift my hands and my heart in total PRAISE to You. You, O God, are worthy of all the praise, all the glory and all the honor. It is in the marvelous and matchless name of Jesus that we pray.

Amen.

Today's Prayer

God is not giving up on you. God still believes in you. God still believes that you are the best option to accomplish His plans. God still knows there is something inside of you worth fighting for. God still desires to show God's strength through your weakness. God sees your purpose in your process. God sees your power through your pain. God even sees what you are trying to hide.... and God wants to use it for His glory.

I wish you could see what God sees... God is not giving up on you. Don't you give up either. I'm praying for you.

Today's Prayer

Some mornings I wake up and I am overcome with just how good God is. I can't always put it into words. Sometimes I just lift my hands and the tears begin to flow. We spend a lot of time asking, wanting, and complaining. But every once in a while, we just need to take a moment and reflect on just how good God is! Think about the doors God has already opened. Think about the "ways" God has already made. This is where your strength to press on lies. Don't just name and claim what you need to happen. Name what has been done. CLAIM that if God did it before. Somebody oughta give God an ALREADY Praise!

God, I thank You for everything You have ALREADY done. I thank You for every mountain You have already moved. I thank You for every blessing You have ALREADY poured into my life. I thank You for the health I ALREADY have. I thank You for the strength I ALREADY have. I thank You for the joy I ALREADY have. God, You have ALREADY done more than we deserve and we just want to say THANK YOU! What is your ALREADY PRAISE?

I dare you to join me and see won't it strengthen your heart and shift your atmosphere!

Today's Prayer

Today, I pray that you will stop measuring your faith by what you see in others. I pray that you will trust that God will use whatever amount of faith YOU have to position you for your purpose. Your mustard seed faith is mountain-moving faith! I decree and declare that your faith has sown good seeds and you WILL reap a harvest of blessings if you don't give up.

I speak into your spirit this morning that you will not give up. You will keep the faith. Not only do you have mountain-moving faith. You have Mountain-Moving-Trouble Trampling-Problem Preventing-Anxiety Alleviating-Trauma Transcending FAITH! And THAT faith says it IS so! In the mighty and matchless name of Jesus Christ!

I'm praying for you.

Today's Prayer

In times like these, you have to stay grounded in your faith. I pray that you will make time to strengthen your relationship with God. When trouble comes, I pray that you will hold fast to what you know for sho'. I speak that when life's storm winds blow, your soul will be anchored in God's truth.

I decree and declare according to God's word that the test won't break you, the lies of the enemy won't shake you and the past can't overtake you ~ because you know God won't forsake you and God's promises await you. Be encouraged. Strengthen what remains. Build on the faith that you have. You will make it through this.

I'm praying for you.

Today's Prayer

I do not recommend that you ONLY use The Message translation of the Bible when studying God's word. I always use several translations for my own understanding ~ even before I go to different commentaries. But every once in a while ~ that "cookies on the lower shelf" translation blesses me! Be Blessed!

Keep a cool head. Stay alert. The Devil is poised to pounce, and would like nothing better than to catch you napping. Keep your guard up. You're not the only ones plunged into these hard times. It's the same with Christians all over the world. So keep a firm grip on the faith. The suffering won't last forever. It won't be long before this generous God who has great plans for us in Christ— eternal and glorious plans they are! —will have you put together and on your feet for good. He gets the last word; yes, he does. (1 Peter 5:8-11 MSG)

God, I pray that you will keep us calm and alert during these trying times. The enemy is on the prowl but we speak that we are covered by Your grace and he won't catch us napping, slipping, or lunching. We are grateful to know that we are not alone in times like these. Help us to lift each other, help us to hold tight to our faith knowing that this suffering won't last forever.

Your Word says You WILL protect us. Your word says You WILL prosper us. Your Word says You WILL give us peace. Your Word is Your plan and Your plans for us WILL manifest in the name of Jesus. Thanks be to God that we serve a God who spoke the first word and always gets the last word! We come into agreement with Your Word and call it to be so! In the name of the One who rose from the grave with the last word.

In Jesus' name, Amen.

Today's Prayer

Woke up at 2:22 am and felt really tense. Started thinking of all I needed to get done today and I could feel my body/muscles getting tight. I could feel the stress. My instinct was to jump up and go into a warfare prayer. Worshipping in unknown tongues until I'm drained. Yelling in prayer at a God who is not deaf. *(This is what Karren does often ~ I ain't slick checking)* But I heard: *Relax.*

I regulated my breathing and spoke peace to my body. When I woke up again, I felt well-rested. Looked at my phone and a friend had texted: I'm praying for you. I am so grateful that God loves us enough to send rest to the weary and intercessors for the intercessors. Now I have the strength to pray for YOU. I'll still probably pray really loud at some point, but not because God can't hear me. Simply because sometimes that's how my voice reacts when I express the passion I have for Christ in the presence of the power of the Holy Spirit. Jeremiah said it's like FIRE...

God, thank you for knowing what we need when we need it. I pray that my friend reading this will trust that You know best ~ even when the divine solution is different from what's normal. I speak PEACE to those who are pushing through stressful situations. I speak PEACE to those who are attempting to manage chaos. I speak PEACE to those who are fighting battles that only God can win. God, sometimes we are so conditioned to fight that we don't realize when we've stepped in front of You during the battle. Lord give us the wisdom and the courage to take a step back and experience Your Peace while You fight our battles. PEACE. BE STILL. VICTORY is OURS. I pray this prayer in the name of the One who gave us HIS peace. His name is Jesus.

Amen.

Today's Prayer

God is releasing creativity. Write down every idea you have ~ even if they don't make sense. Understand that the world is shifting and God is speaking into your future. God is speaking divine creativity for a world that we don't know as normal yet. Start writing. Start planning. It WILL make sense. God is leveling the playing field before God releases the blessing. And YOU are becoming who you need to be to SUSTAIN the blessing. Be ready when God says GO!

I'm praying for you.

Today's Prayer

Praying for those who believe yet still need help with their unbelief. I pray that YOU will begin to pray God's word over your fear and your anxiety as you show strength but feel weak. I decree that what you already know about God will add comfort and not confusion. Speak what YOU know. You already know God to be a protector. You already know God to be a healer. You already know God to be a miracle worker. I declare that you will speak what you know and as you hear YOU say what YOU know ~ your faith will be increased daily. I decree it. I declare it. And it is so.

I'm praying for you.

Today's Prayer

God answered you. Stop second-guessing what you heard just because it's uncomfortable. Take the first step. Start the conversation. God knows you're nervous about it. God will be with you. God told Joshua "be strong and courageous" THREE times ~ so either he was having second thoughts or he was trying to "LOGIC" his way out of what God said. *(yeah, sounds like you, huh?)* God told him, *Be obedient and you will have success. Do what I said and you will be prosperous and successful.* Most importantly, God promised to be with him wherever he went.

My prayer for you is that you will be strong and courageous. I release divine courage for you to step out on faith and do what God said. In your obedience, I decree success and prosperity according to God's word. Because God said so, I declare that God will be with you WHEREVER you go! I speak it and it so, in the name and authority of Jesus, and by the power of His shed blood.

Amen and Amen.

Today's Prayer

Reading the word of God helps me to hear a Word FROM God. God STILL speaks through what God already said. God's word is STILL valid. God's word STILL applies. Your situation is new to YOU ~ it's not new to God.

God, I'm praying for the one who needs to hear a word from You. I pray that they can find their courage from Esther for such a time as this. I pray they discover the hope of healing from the woman with the issue of blood. I speak that they will learn "it ain't over until God says it's over" from Jairus' daughter. I pray they can trace Your hand on their life like Joseph from the pit to the palace and even know that sometimes You will anoint us long before You elevate us like David. I pray they discover the power of Your protection from reading about Daniel in the Lion's Den or the three Hebrew boys. I pray they find and receive Your forgiveness like the woman caught in adultery. I pray they learn to run and tell about Your goodness like the Samaritan woman at the well.

And I pray that they never forget to say Thank You like the one leper who came back to Jesus. God, we thank you for giving us the Basic Instructions Before Leaving Earth (BIBLE)! Now we ask that you help us to seek and understand how to follow instructions. Reacquaint us with Your Word so that we can realign with Your will. I pray this prayer in the name of the One whose words and actions continue to teach us and draw us nearer to You. His name is Jesus.

Amen and Amen.

Today's Prayer

God is on your side. God is working on your behalf. Anchor yourself in God's word. Immerse yourself in prayer. You are not outnumbered. You have not run out of grace. God hears you. God will show up. God will deliver. You + God = The Majority. Victory belongs to you. Repeat it. Receive it.

I'm praying for you.

Today's Prayer

So Jacob was left alone, and a man wrestled with him till daybreak. When the man saw that he could not overpower him, he touched the socket of Jacob's hip so that his hip was wrenched as he wrestled with the man. Then the man said, "Let me go, for it is daybreak." But Jacob replied, "I will not let you go unless you bless me." The man asked him, "What is your name?" "Jacob," he answered. Then the man said, "Your name will no longer be Jacob, but Israel, because you have struggled with God and with humans and have overcome."
(Genesis 32:24-28 NIV)

There is a PRAISE in the atmosphere! You've been wrestling like Jacob. You've been determined like Jacob. God is about to change what "they" call you because you have wrestled and overcome! Give God praise in advance! Turn to your neighbor and say "I WON'T LET GO TIL YOU BLESS ME!" Hold on friends…I'm praying for you and praising with you!

Today's Prayer

Praying for the ones who are at the end of their patience and are about to take matters into their own hands.

God, I pray that You would let them feel Your presence today. Give them the blessed assurance that You are still with them and You are still working on their behalf. Because right now it doesn't feel like it and it doesn't look like it. I pray that You will align their "right time" with Your right time. And while they wait, I speak that You will COMFORT them with Your peace. ENCOURAGE them with Your presence. STRENGTHEN them to be able to trust You when they can't trace You. I offer this prayer in the name and authority of Jesus Christ.

Amen and Amen.

Today's Prayer

Give your entire attention to what God is doing right now, and don't get worked up about what may or may not happen tomorrow. God will help you deal with whatever hard things come up when the time comes.

(Matthew 6:34 MSG)

Learn to STOP creating anxiety. There are enough things to be anxious about without you manufacturing anticipatory anxiety. You are worrying about things that you have imagined COULD happen. Your body does not always know it's your imagination. So your body goes into fight, flight, or freeze mode but NOTHING is happening right now. You say you believe that the weapons may form but they will NOT prosper. But you're still nervous about them forming? Most times when it comes to anxiety, YOU are the one forming the weapon. Heart racing. Head hurting. Tears flowing. Ain't nothing happening. Give your attention to what God is doing right now.

Right now you are safe.

Right now you are healthy.

Right now you are calm.

Strategy for your future and stressing for your future are two different things. Catch yourself today when you worry about what COULD happen.

Whisper: *All is well. I am safe. I am healthy. I am calm. I am present in my present.*

I'm praying for you.

Today's Prayer

I am realizing that many of us know how to ASK in prayer but we don't always know how to respond. We keep trying to find different ways to pray to get the answer we want. Yet, we haven't responded to what God has spoken to us during our prayer time. God is waiting on your YES. We can't just expect God to bless irrespective of our actions. Do your part. Hold up your end of the bargain. God desires to bless you. God is waiting on you to LIVE your YES. Say it AND live it. I pray as you enjoy a worship experience today that you will hear God clearly through a song or a sermon and you will respond with your YES.

I'm praying for you.

Today's Prayer

Do not conform to the pattern of this world, but be transformed by the renewing of your mind. THEN you will be able to test and approve what God's will is - His good, pleasing and perfect will.

(Romans 12:2 NIV)

We quote the 1st part of that verse *(renewing of the mind)*, but we leave off the 2nd half *(the ability to discern God's will)*. Today, I pray you will receive the 2nd half of God's Word. I speak that what you have come through in your first half has TRANSFORMED you and brought you closer to God. Therefore, in the second half, you will be able to DISCERN God's will. I speak that you will be able to hear God's voice above a whisper. I speak CLARITY in your hearing and DETERMINATION in your moving.

No more second-guessing. No more questioning. God is FOR you ~ on the mountain or in the valley. May peace and favor rest on your house in the 2nd half. May grace and mercy follow you in the 2nd half. For THIS 2nd half, may your latter be greater in the name of Jesus! I offer this prayer in the name and authority of Jesus Christ and by the power of His shed blood. It is so!

Amen and Amen.

Today's Prayer

DON'T COMPROMISE. To compromise means to accept standards that are lower than desirable. It is the result of a settlement. It is giving up something because you don't believe you can have all of what you're asking for or all of what you need.

The two reasons I got for your desire to compromise were:

1) You don't think you can wait on what God promised.

2) You don't think you are worth what God promised.

Whatever you are considering compromising right now is going to affect your future and the time that it will take for you to reach the FULL MANIFESTATION of God's promise for your life.

Don't delay your destiny.

Don't compromise.

I'm praying for you.

Today's Prayer

Today, I will activate my faith and come into alignment with God's YES. I will not second-guess God or question God's favor in my situation.

Today, I will activate my faith and come into alignment with God's YES. I will no longer pray for God's divine purpose and then deny God's determined plan.

Today, I will activate my faith and come into alignment with God's YES. I will not speak God's word as a seed in my situation and then kill the seed in the next breath by speaking doubt.

Today, I will activate my faith and come into alignment with God's YES. God loves me enough to work this matter for my good and I will trust God enough to let it be so.

My faith is activated.
I have God's permission.
It is settled in my spirit.
It will manifest in my life.
I speak it and it IS so!
In Jesus' name, Amen.

Today's Prayer

You have not disqualified yourself from God's plan for you. God is still working things together for the fulfillment of God's plan and God still wants to use you to do it. Your mistakes have not disqualified you. Stop wallowing in self-pity. It's time to MOVE through the shadows of your bad decisions. Allow God to shine God's light of forgiveness on you. Your past has not disqualified you. God has already forgiven what you can't seem to forget. Stop the enemy's replay in your mind and receive the freedom of God's grace and mercy. Release the pain of the past and return to God's path for YOU! You are not banned, disbarred, ineligible, eliminated, or out of the running.

God's grace is sufficient. You will have what God promised. You will come out of this darkness. You will come through this storm. You will get over this mountain. You are forgiven. You will see the goodness of the Lord. The One who has begun a good work in YOU will complete it. And it IS so!

In the mighty and matchless name of Jesus.

Today's Prayer

Cast your burden on the Lord, and he will sustain you; he will never permit the righteous to be moved. (Psalm 55:22 NRSV)

God, I thank You that I can give You my burdens and my issues. I ask right now that You would help me to discern the things that burden me so that I'm not trying to fight through situations and emotions that You are waiting to handle for me. Help me, O God, to know the battles that belong to You! God my desire is to rest in the truth that You will sustain me. You promised to strengthen and support me, to comfort me and to carry me through. Help me to find peace in Your promise ~ even when I can't find peace in the process. This process is hard, God.

But as I go through, don't allow me to be moved from Your will. Don't let the trouble shake my faith to the point where it takes my joy. I stand on Your word that says You will not allow the righteous to be moved. And I rejoice in the fact that even with all of my faults- even with all of the mistakes I've made ~ Your grace and Your mercy still call me righteous. Today I will give you my problems. Today You will sustain me. Today I will not be moved. I speak it and it is so.

In Jesus' name, Amen.

Today's Prayer

Ask for forgiveness. Receive Forgiveness. Walk in Forgiveness.

I'm praying for the ones who are having difficulty receiving forgiveness. God brought this song back to me. Ask for forgiveness. Receive Forgiveness. Walk in Forgiveness. The enemy is using guilt and shame to keep you stagnant. Your next move is clouded by your own thoughts of what you don't deserve from God because of what you didn't do (or what you did).

God is attempting to order your steps but you won't move your feet because YOU can't forget the wrong that God has already forgiven. God desires to do a new thing but you won't stop beating yourself up for the old thing. It happened. You did it. Admit it. God is offering you another chance.

I'm praying for you.

Today's Prayer

Whatever you are facing and whatever you are fighting, God's grace is sufficient!

GRACE: unmerited favor.

UNMERITED: not earned or deserved.

FAVOR: approval, support, kindness beyond what is due.

SUFFICIENT: enough, abundant.

Affirmation: *I am grateful that God's grace is sufficient for (state your issue).*

God, I thank You that Your grace is sufficient for me. I am grateful that as I depend on You, You show me the support that I did not earn; approval I do not deserve and kindness beyond what I am due. Thank you, God, for your unmerited favor! Your grace is always enough for my situation. I can remain confident in You because even when I don't know how long trouble will last, I do know that Your grace is abundant and does not run out. Your grace has kept me safe thus far and Your grace will lead me on. Thank you for your Amazing Grace.

Hallelujah and Amen!

Today's Prayer

Thank you for your love. Thank you for your power. Thank you for protection - every hour!

Whenever your faith is shaky, start thanking God for what God has already done. Think about God's faithfulness in your life. When your faith is shaky don't just say "God I thank you for everything" take the time to "count" your blessings. Name them. Every time you THINK ~ THANK!!

God's timing is not our timing but I have learned that the wait is easier when you are grateful. So today, thank God in everything and for everything. As soon as something happens, I even challenge you to say, "Thank you God" or "Thank you Jesus" out loud *(like Big Momma used to do)*. I promise it will shift your faith perspective. Oh, and today I thank God for using these reflections to strengthen your heart, increase your faith and answer your prayers. I am forever grateful.

Thank you, Lord!

Today's Prayer

Morning Worship + Prayer + Your declaration for today.

Even when I don't see it ~ You're working. Even when I don't feel it ~ You're working. You never stop. You never stop working. Way Maker. Miracle Worker. Promise Keeper. Light in the darkness. That is who You are.

God, I am so grateful that you NEVER stop working! You are a God who never sleeps or slumbers. You are a God who keeps promises. You are a God who is faithful. While I'm trying to figure it out ~ You have already worked it out! In quarantine ~ you're working. Under curfew -you're working! I bless You because you are a WONDER WORKING GOD! I praise you in advance for working it out for me.

I praise you right now for working all things for my good. You never stop. You never stop working. I'll never stop. I'll never stop PRAISING! Thank you, God that I can start my day and join You in Your work. I pray this prayer to the One who will complete the work that He has begun until the day Jesus returns. Hallelujah and Amen.

Now take a moment, fill in the blank, and declare this ALL DAY:

Even when I'm _____, You're working!

Today's Prayer

Sometimes you hear God clearly. Sometimes you know exactly what you are supposed to change. Sometimes you just don't want to do it. Sometimes you weigh out how much the change will shift your life or your relationship or your income and decide you don't want to lose what God is trying to get you to give up. Sometimes you aren't waiting on God's answer ~ you are waiting on God to give you a Plan B. If this is one of those times, here is the prayer: "God help me to do what is RIGHT not what is easy."

God's wisdom is not multiple choice. He said what He said.

I'm praying for you.

Today's Prayer

1 Corinthians 15:58

Therefore, my beloved brethren, be steadfast, immovable, always abounding in the work of the Lord, knowing that your labor is not in vain in the Lord. (NKJV)

With all this going for us, my dear, dear friends, stand your ground. And don't hold back. Throw yourselves into the work of the Master, confident that nothing you do for him is a waste of time or effort. (MSG)

STEADFAST: firm in belief, determination, or adherence; loyal.

IMMOVABLE: used to describe a firm opinion that is impossible to change.

God, I decree according to Your Word that in this season we will be STEADFAST. I speak that we will be firm in our belief OF healing, peace and justice. We will be determined in our faithfulness and loyalty to the one true and living God. I declare according to Your Word that we will be IMMOVABLE. I speak that we will continue to have a firm opinion aligned with the Word of God. Our faith will be impossible to change because we have faith in a God who does not change.

We will abound! I speak an overflow in the name of Jesus! We will abound in favor. We will abound in anointing. We will abound in wisdom. And with all of this going for us ~ we will STAND OUR GROUND with complete confidence, knowing that what we do for God is never a waste of time or effort. I speak it and it is so! In the matchless name of Jesus, Amen.

Today's Prayer

God gives strength for the wait. We are all waiting on something. Something to start, something to stop, something to move, something to be answered... waiting on a cure, waiting on justice... I was tired yesterday and my prayers reflected my truth.

This morning I read Psalm 27 and verse 14 stood out for me:

Wait on the Lord; Be of good courage, And He shall strengthen your heart; Wait, I say, on the Lord! (NKJV)

Stay with God! Take heart. Don't quit. I'll say it again: Stay with God. (MSG)

Today's Prayer

God, help me and my sisters and brothers who are reading this prayer to wait WITH YOU. God, you know us. We are impatient. We get tired of waiting. But we believe in Your Word that says if we have the courage to wait WITH You ~ You will strengthen our hearts. We decree according to Your Word that our ability to wait is increased because we choose to wait on the plans of our Divine Creator.

You are a miracle-working God and for that, we give You praise. Yet, even more than that, You are a God who sustains Your people. For that, we bless Your Holy Name. We will still rejoice over the sweatless victories, but we will also wait and work for those that require our sweat and our tears.

We will wait on You... because You know the plans.

We will wait on You... because You made the promise.

God, we will wait on You because You have the POWER to bring the plans and the promises to pass! Whatever plan you showed us ~ it is so! Whatever promise you whispered in our hearts ~ it is so! Strengthen us, O God, for the wait. Equip us for the long haul. Help us to hold up and to hold on. And we will remain confident in this: We WILL see the goodness of the Lord! We pray this prayer in the name of the One who is the author and the finisher of our faith. His name is Jesus.

Amen and Amen.

Today's Prayer

God, I pray that You would help me to let go of the anxieties of yesterday and not pick up the anxieties for tomorrow. In the name and authority of Jesus and by the power of His shed blood, I will live in the present and in the presence of God's favor on this day. God, I speak that you will give me the power to take captive every thought, emotion and imagination that does not align with your word or your will. God bring my mind, body and soul in alignment with your promises of health, protection and prosperity. Thank you, God, for being an ever-present help in the time of trouble. I love you. I honor you. I bless Your holy name. It is in the name of Jesus that I pray and give thanks.

Hallelujah and Amen.

Today's Prayer

Praying for the ones who have seen so much and survived so much that sometimes they don't think CHANGE is coming. They can't envision change in the world and definitely can't see change in their own situations. God help us not to settle for less than what you have designed for our lives. Even with crisis on top of crisis, I still believe that You O God are going to come through. I bind every trick, plan and scheme of the enemy to keep us frustrated and tied to the past. I loose the power of God's truth in our lives. The truth that we don't have to lie dormant in our mistakes. The truth that we can have what we speak. The truth that nothing is impossible with God. The truth that You love us and are FOR US. The truth that when You are FOR us nothing can stand against us.

Help us to receive the power of the Word of God to set us FREE. Free to do our part. Free to align our efforts with the strategic plan of God. THEN the manifestations of God's divine favor will overtake us. THEN God will hear from heaven and heal the land. THEN God will shift our situations and work them for our good. Help us God to be faithful until THEN.... I offer this prayer in the name of the One who died for our change. His name is Jesus.

Amen and Amen.

Today's Prayer

I am grateful that I serve a God who sees the end from the beginning. The Divine Creator who is the author and finisher of my faith. Which means God came up with the plan and God has the power to bring it to pass. THIS is the God I serve. I serve a God who is not scrambling when trouble comes. My God is not surprised and coming up with a strategy when a pandemic hits. My God knows all, sees all, and is my all and all. THIS is the God I serve.

I serve a God whose name is above all names. I serve a God who speaks and it is so. I serve a God who makes rough places smooth, high places low, and crooked places straight. I serve a God who helps and heals, who directs and delivers, who promises and protects, who endows then endorses, who SAYS it and SETTLES it! THIS is the God I serve. I serve a God who is ABLE and there is NOTHING too hard for my God! I give God all the glory, honor and praise.

Hallelujah!

Today's Prayer

Praying for the ones who are trying to be STRONG for others. Still trying to "look" in control because you believe that if YOU lose it- every thing and every one else will fall apart. I get it. "Strong" is how you move in the earth and you don't know how NOT to do it. I get it because I am YOU.

My hope is that you find a moment and a safe space to release. I am praying that you don't implode while you are trying not to explode. I know your family/friends need you and expect a LOT from you. I pray that you point them towards Jesus so that you can stop being their savior. I'm praying for US!

Love y'all for real.

Today's Prayer

How long will you waver between two opinions? It's time to make a decision. You have stalled long enough. You have all of the information you need. You've seen all you need to see. This is where your FAITH comes in. Either you are going to trust God or you are not. Either you are going to move in faith or sit in doubt.

See, you want God to make the decision for you. Ain't no faith in that. Trust God. Don't depend on your understanding of comfort and safety. Accept God's Sovereignty. Accept God's love for you. Make the decision. Take the step. Watch God lead you ...after you start moving. I'm praying these Scriptures for you. Read them and pray them for yourself as well.

⁵ Trust in the Lord with all your heart, And lean not on your own understanding; ⁶In all your ways acknowledge Him, And He shall direct your paths. (Proverbs 3:5-6 NKJV)

²¹ Your ears shall hear a word behind you, saying, "This is the way, walk in it," Whenever you turn to the right hand Or whenever you turn to the left. (Isaiah 30:21 NKJV)

³¹ So whether you eat or drink or whatever you do, do it all for the glory of God. (1 Corinthians 10:31 NIV)

Today's Prayer

Your praise shifts the atmosphere. It takes your eyes off of your problems and places them on the One who promised you peace and provision. Reading Psalm 34 this morning shifted my eyes and my spirit. I have included a few verses and a prayer. It might be long cause I got caught up. Read every bit of it OUT LOUD...maybe you will get "caught up" too! I love y'all for real ~ now come on and BLESS the Lord with me!

I will bless the Lord at all times; His praise shall continually be in my mouth. My soul shall make its boast in the Lord; The humble shall hear of it and be glad. Oh, magnify the Lord with me, And let us exalt His name together. I sought the Lord, and He heard me, And delivered me from all my fears. (Psalm 34:1-4 NKJV)

God, I bless you. God, I love you. God, I lift you! I lift your name above all others. I lift your plan above my own. You are worthy to be praised! From the rising of the sun until the going down of the same. I will give you praise. When I don't feel like it ~ I will praise you until I do. You have been good. You ARE good and your mercies endure forever.

Thank you for keeping me. Thank you for never leaving me. Thank you for choosing me. Thank you for using me. If I had ten thousand tongues, I couldn't thank you enough! Thank you for every open door. Thank you for every closed door. Thank you for leading me when I didn't want to be lead. Thank you for looking beyond my faults and not just seeing but MEETING my every need.

I give you ALL the glory! I give you ALL the honor! I give you ALL the praise! Hallelujah! Hallelujah!

Hallelujah and Amen!

Today's Prayer

Affirmation:

I have been saved by grace. I have been justified by faith. I am completely secure in God; nothing will be able to separate me from God's love in Christ Jesus. No one is able to snatch me out of God's hand. The peace of God guards my heart. God will never leave me nor forsake me. I believe it to be so.

Read it again out loud. Take a deep breath at the periods.

I have been saved by grace.

I have been justified by faith.

I am completely secure in God; nothing will be able to separate me from God's love in Christ Jesus.

No one is able to snatch me out of God's hand.

The peace of God guards my heart.

God will never leave me nor forsake me.

I believe it to be so.

I pray your faith is increased as you hear YOU read God's word concerning you.

Today's Prayer

You've got too many loose ends. You need to finish some stuff and end some stuff so that God can release the new stuff. I don't mean just turn your back and let it fade away. I mean, face it and finish it! Muster up whatever energy, strength, or courage you need to. But get it done. Whatever "it" is ~ it will not go away on its own. It will lie dormant and resurface to distract you later. Finish the project. Have the conversation. End the relationship. I don't know what it is...but this up and down and back and forth is delaying the FULL manifestation of God's purpose in your life.

As you are reading this, you know exactly what or who "it" is.

Handle it.

God has more for you.

I'm praying for you.

Today's Prayer

For everything that was written in the past was written to teach us, so that through the ENDURANCE taught in the Scriptures and the ENCOURAGEMENT they provide we might have HOPE.
(Romans 15:4 NIV)

My great grandmother used the word HOPE for HELP. As an adult, sometimes they mean the same thing for me. So, this morning I pray that God would HOPE us.

Lord, send us Your HOPE and send us Your HELP! God, we are seeking your face and leaning on Your Word. I speak that you will endow us with the divine endurance that is taught in the Scriptures. I decree according to Your Word, that even in this season of racial turmoil and emotional turbulence, we will receive the encouragement offered through the Holy Scriptures.

In the midst of it all, we receive the peace that is beyond our understanding. In the midst of it all, we receive the joy that we can't find the words to explain. In the midst of it all, we will continue to walk in the divine wisdom that leads us to the fulfillment of Your promises. In the midst of it all, we speak HOPE in the name of Jesus! I pray this prayer to the Triune ONE who knows all, sees all and conquers all! In the name of the Father, the Son and the Holy Spirit.

Amen and Amen.

Today's Prayer

Open your mind today. God has a blessing for you that is outside of your norm. Don't dismiss God's favor or instructions just because it's not the way you have seen God show up in the past. You've been praying for 'a new thing' so why do you think it will look or feel like the 'old' thing? God is sending NEW. God is sending DIFFERENT. You will never grow if you keep rejecting uncomfortable opportunities. In this season of uncertainty, God is showing up in uncommon, unusual, unlikely and unthinkable ways.

Open your mind.

Don't miss the move of God.

I speak Uncommon blessings ... Unusual favor ... Unlikely connections ... Unthinkable joy ... I speak it and it IS so!

I'm praying for you.

Today's Prayer

*"The Lord bless you
and keep you;
the Lord make his face shine on you
and be gracious to you;
the Lord turn his face toward you
and give you peace."*

(Numbers 6:24-26 NIV)

    This morning God, I just want to speak a blessing over my friend who is reading this. I pray that You would bless them. Bless them in their coming and their going. Give them what they need physically, spiritually, mentally and financially. God, I pray for their protection. You, O God, are a Keeper! Keep them safe. Keep them well. Keep them as they dwell in the secret place of the Most High. Keep them as they press forward from day to day. God, I believe they believe in You and I ask that you keep them as they work through their unbelief.

    Shine the light of Your glory on them God. Smile on my friend. Let them see You in their situation and know that because You are present ~ it WILL work out. Be gracious to them God. Times are hard. Bills are due. Life just isn't what it was. I speak Your divine grace over them in the name of Jesus.

    God, turn Your face toward them. Let them know that they are seen by You ~ that You know their issues and their struggles. Let them know that You love them the way they are but You love them too much to just let them stay that way! God please send Your peace to my friend.

    Peace from Your promise.

    Peace in the process.

    Peace as they prosper.

    This is my prayer.

    In Jesus' name. Amen.

Today's Prayer

The LORD is close to the brokenhearted and saves those who are crushed in spirit. Praying for those whose hearts have been broken...
(Psalm 34:18)

Speaking comfort over those whose spirits have been crushed. Come close God. Allow us to feel your presence. In your presence is fullness of joy. I speak a restored joy for those who are grieving. God shall wipe all of our tears away.

I'm praying for us.

Today's Prayer

We often put too many demands on ourselves when we are stressed which causes us more stress. Today I am praying for those who are stressed and stretched. I decided to share some affirmations I wrote for me during my prayer time. Take deep breaths as you read them. You will make it through. We will make it through. I'm praying for you.

Today I will be kinder to myself.
Today I will show myself more compassion.
Today I will give myself a break.
Today I will allow others to hold their own anxiety.
Today I will be mindful of my emotions.
Today I will become more and more calm with every deep breath I take.
Today I will rid my mind of undue expectations.
Today I will feel good if I answer every phone call.
Today I will feel good if I choose not to answer every phone call.
Today I will stay present in the moment.
Today I will feel what I feel and be okay.
God is near. God is in control. I am safe in God's presence.

Today's Prayer

When peace like a river, attendeth my way,
When sorrows like sea billows roll:
Whatever my lot, Thou hast taught me to know
It is well, it is well, with my soul.
~It Is Well With My Soul (Horatio Spatford 1873)

With everything that's going on in the world, God we thank you for moments of peace. Thank you that Your peace LITERALLY surpasses our understanding. Even as we are once again painfully reminded of your Sovereignty ~ God I thank you that Your Word brings us peace and comfort. It's easy to pray when it hurts- as long as it doesn't hurt you. But even in the hurt, God, I thank you for the Strength to pray THROUGH. God, I thank You for a faith that endures the storm. I thank You that YOUR WORD IS TRUE, and Your strength is being made perfect in this time of weakness. God, we put our faith in You. You alone bring peace in the storm. You alone bring joy in sorrow. You alone are God and You are God alone. Thank You for the strength to say by faith that it is well with my soul.

Today's Prayer

When I was praying that God would answer the prayers of His people, this is what I heard: *I hear them praying. Many don't have room for me. They pray for a new thing but all they really want is more of what they have always had.*

So now my prayer is that we will make room for God. That we will have the courage to unlearn some of the things we "know" so that we can know God more fully. I pray that we can detach ourselves from some of our accomplishments so that we can attach ourselves to the rest of God's plan for our lives. We have to stop fitting God into our box of "success." Take the limits off of your dreams. Remove the familiar boundaries from your goals. Stop trying to reproduce what you've always seen. Allow God to show you YOUR new and YOUR next.

God's ways are higher.
God's thoughts are higher.
It's time for you to go higher.
I'm praying for you.

Today's Prayer

"If it had not been for the Lord who was on our side,"
(Psalm 124:1 NKJV)

Thank you, Lord, for knowing I could not handle what I was praying for. Thank you, Lord, for blocking it. Thank you, Lord, for removing it. Thank you, Lord, for saying it would not be so.

Thank you, Lord, for telling the enemy NO. Thank you, Lord, for saving me from myself. Thank you, Lord, for closed doors.

Thank you, Lord, for ending unhealthy relationships that I never would have ended myself.

Thank you, Lord, for the delay that gave me time to focus.

Thank you, Lord, for the setback that gave me time to regroup.

Thank you, Lord, for the detour that let me avoid needless tears and wasted years.

I would have lost it all.
I would have jacked it up.
I would have aborted the plan.
I would have surrendered my birthright.
I would have sacrificed my purpose.
If it had not been for the Lord who was on our side…
God, I thank You!

Today's Prayer

Lately, God has been changing your mind and your heart about a lot of things. Please don't allow people to bully you or shame you out of the change God is making in your life. You have become too concerned about what "they" might say. "They" are going to talk about you anyway. So let it be about God's favor and not your fear. You've been praying too hard and waiting too long to allow the opinions of others to delay your breakthrough OR your blessing! They may not understand your shift and it's okay. Stop fighting. Stop defending. Move with grace and humility. Pray for them and allow God to bring them along in God's time. This is your time. Stop telling God NO because you want a consensus.

I'm praying for you.

Today's Prayer

Yesterday, I made a logical decision based on fear. 90% of the world would have done the same thing in the same situation. But afterward, I realized I was attempting to control the outcome of the situation and not trusting God to work it out for my good. After I made the decision my spirit was so heavy. I could physically feel the heaviness. I couldn't concentrate on anything and I could not "rationalize" away what I had done. I prayed and repented. The feeling didn't leave. I had to literally go back and UNDO what I had done.

Today, I am praying that you continue to make decisions based on faith and not fear. Fear will show you everything you will lose if it doesn't go your way. But faith will show you everything you will gain if you allow God to have control. I pray that faith will keep you in God's will and walking according to God's purpose for your life. Even when your plan makes sense and puts you on top (according to the world's standards), I speak that you will feel a nagging in your spirit to remind you that God's ways are higher than your ways and God's thoughts are higher than your thoughts.

I decree according to the word of God that as you follow God, things will work out for your good. I speak that doors will open to opportunities that you didn't know existed. I speak that divine provision will come that will be greater than what you projected in your fear. So, if God says UNDO something- undo it. If God says stop trying to control a situation -STOP. Trust God and know that YOUR safest place is in the will of God.

It's tight but it's right. I'm praying for you.

Today's Prayer

God, we are believing in the new season that you promised. Help us to release the old and receive the new. Old things must pass away. Old habits cannot enter this new season. Old grudges cannot enter this new season. God, we thank you for releasing a new order and a new outlook. In this new season, I speak a sharper discernment.

I speak clarity in the name of Jesus. I speak a new way to deal with old issues. A fresh outlook on old circumstances. The answer will come in the new season. The solution is revealed in the new season. No more confusion and second-guessing. No more comparing what we had to what we have.

God set our faces like flint toward what you have promised! Free us from the things we can't let go of by ourselves. We trust you, God. We believe that Your NEW is better than our old. We believe that Your NEW is better than our comfort. Help us to perceive the new thing. Help us to receive the new thing. Help us to believe the new thing. And Help us to achieve the new thing. We ask all of this in the name of the One who gave His life so that we could be made new.

In Jesus' name, Amen.

Today's Prayer

This morning I couldn't move past the word FOCUS. I believe God is moving and we are missing some details. God's best work is in the details. God's guidance can be found in the details. There is a lot going on and we are too quick to dismiss what we don't understand in an effort to move toward what's comfortable. Pay attention. Pause. Focus.

I speak that God will focus your eyes so that you will see God working for you. I pray that God will decrease the noise in your life so that you can focus on hearing the still, small voice. I decree that every decision will be based on God's direction. No more avoiding. No more neglecting. No more coasting. Pay attention. Pause. Focus.

Your destiny is waiting. I'm praying for you.

Today's Prayer

As I prayed this morning, I asked God, "What do you want me to tell your people." I heard: *I AM STILL IN CONTROL.*

I pray that this Scripture and prayer will give you comfort and strengthen your resolve to speak and believe that God is still in control. I'm praying for you.

So do not fear, for I am with you; do not be dismayed, for I am your God. I will strengthen you and help you; I will uphold you with my righteous right hand. (Isaiah 41:10 NIV)

DISMAY: sudden or complete loss of courage because of some unwelcome situation or occurrence; disheartened.

God, increase my faith to know that You are still in control. I will not lose courage. I will not be disheartened. God is still in control. God will still strengthen and help me. God will still hold me up with God's righteous and victorious hand. Just because the situation is out of MY control ~ it doesn't mean it is out of God's control. God is with me. I will not fear. God is STILL in control.

Thank You for being my refuge. Thank You for being my strong tower. Thank You for not turning me over to my own plan. Thank You for not leaving me when my actions said I had already left You. God is with me. I will not fear. God is still in control.

Today's Prayer

Praying for the ones who have faith but facing anxiety EVERY day is causing doubt. You are not doubting if God can do it ~ but just wondering if God will actually do it FOR YOU. You believe that God is still able but everything you see and feel has started to weigh on you. You are fighting the good fight of faith, but your circumstances are making you battle weary. Please know that your situation does not change who God is. Align your thoughts and words with who God IS! Believe by faith. Speak with faith. Walk by faith. I pray today that your faith will be increased as you decree and declare the names of God, the character of God and the power of God. God is still able. God will still do it for you. I'm praying for you.

Declaration *(speak aloud)*:

God, I thank you for being El Roi (ROW-eye) the One who Sees me.

God, I thank you for being Jehovah Rophe (RAH-fah) the God who Heals me.

God, I thank you for being Jehovah Jireh (JI-rah) the God who Provides for me.

God, I thank you for being Jehovah Shalom the God who gives me Peace.

I believe that God is still able, and I believe that God will do it for me.

I believe that God is still able, and I believe that God will do it for me.

I believe that God is still able, and I believe that God will do it for me.

Today's Prayer

God loves you. You will get through this. You have faced bigger mountains before. You have overcome before. You have been healed before. You have survived before. Think about it. Pull out your victory receipts! Pull out your faith receipts! I bind thoughts of defeat and despair and I speak strength and power to your spirit right now in the name of Jesus.

I decree and declare that you will begin to take your "all over the place" thoughts captive and align them with the word of God. Remember and reflect on the times God came through for you. Reflect on the times YOU came through for you.

Now take a deep breath. Slow down.

Your race. Your pace.

God loves you.

You will get through this night. This week. This year.

I'm praying for you.

Today's Prayer

God has been putting ideas in YOUR spirit and guiding you toward habits and goals that you don't fully understand. I pray that you won't lean to your own understanding but that you would just trust God and be obedient. You keep praying for God's promises to manifest ~ but you won't allow God to prepare you. You won't allow God to increase your discipline. If God is waking you up consistently at 3am, it is not for you to watch Netflix until you drift back off to sleep. If God is removing people from your life, it is not for you to chase them and see why they don't want to be around you anymore. God is preparing you in THIS season for the promises God is sending for the NEXT season.

I speak that as you surrender you will have peace in your preparation and a divine dispensation of power as you walk into your purpose. And it is so ~ according to the promises of God's Word.

I'm praying for you.

Today's Prayer

Just because God has not done it ~ doesn't mean God is not able to do it. The fact that the mountain has not moved ~ does not signify a lack of power on God's part. Neither does it convey God's absence from your situation or a disregard for your pain. Jesus said keep asking, keep seeking, keep knocking. Our faith has become limited and conditional. We are spoiled and want everything when and how we desire.

We even try to use God's word to "force" God's hand. We don't want to learn the lesson: we just want the trouble to stop. *(read that again)* You want the discomfort to end ~ so you pray for God to change "them" or change "it" so that God doesn't have to change YOU. God still works things together for good. God still does exceedingly abundantly more than we can ask or think. God can still bring you out alright!

I decree and declare according to God's word that the testing of your faith will produce perseverance [determination/endurance]. I speak that you will let perseverance finish its work so that you may be mature and complete, not lacking anything. I pray that you won't grow weary because DUE SEASON is on the way.

I love you and I'm praying for you.

Today's Prayer

It's been a hard fight but you can still finish strong. All is not lost. Even through your tears ~ I pray you can see God clearly. God is still blessing even in times of pain. God is still opening doors even in times of trouble. I pray that God moves mightily for you today! I pray that you can recover the MINDSET that allows you to dream and be creative. I pray that you can recover the DETERMINATION that allows you to push through your process and walk into your promise. I pray that you can recover the JOY that allows you to stay grounded in gratitude. The victory may not look like you thought it would, but it does not mean victory is not available. Victory STILL belongs to you.

I'm praying for you.

Today's Prayer

As you walk through your home this morning, plead the blood of Jesus over your home, your family, your property and your purpose. Call each family member by name. Ask God to prepare and protect them on this day and for those to come. Speak life and love throughout your home. As you cover your home, I decree that the angels of protection will go before you today. I speak provision and power for your purpose. I speak an unshakable peace in your spirit that will command peace and order in your presence. God has given you authority! No more wavering in your spirit. No more quivering in your voice. No more shaking in your boots. If there is a disruption, I pray that you will stand in your authority and call forth God's peace. If there is chaos, stand in authority and call forth order.

On this day, I speak that God will do exceedingly and abundantly MORE than you could ask, think or dare to imagine according to the power that is in you. Tap into the power and watch God blow your mind. I speak it and it IS so! In the name of the One who has all power and authority. His name is Jesus.

Amen and Amen.

Today's Prayer

Strengthen us, O God! We are doing our best to wait. We are doing our best to hold on. We are even doing our best to believe ~ but we need your strength. Your word says that you would show yourself strong through our weakness. We speak that over our spirits right now in the name of Jesus. Our strength is in You God. My strength is in YOU! We speak strength and power in our innermost being. Renew the spaces in our hearts where we have allowed fear to run rampant. Mend those places God and seal them with Your love. Create clean and pure hearts in us and renew a right and steadfast spirit.

It is getting harder to smile through the pain. So God we ask, like David, that you restore the joy of your salvation and grant us a willing spirit, to sustain us through these times. We will make it through. We will make it over. We will make it out alright! We speak it and it so! Strength and power rest on us.

In Jesus' name, Amen and Amen.

Today's Prayer

God is saying, "LISTEN." You are so busy defending and explaining why you "can't" that you are missing the instructions on how you CAN. LISTEN. Your fear of failure has you trying to look good where you are, while God is sending instructions to change your mental and financial (maybe even your physical) locations. LISTEN.

Shining HERE is easy... but outshining mediocrity is not God's plan for you. Congratulations. You've become the best swimmer in the kiddie pool. Now what? LISTEN. God is speaking. This is not the end of what God has for you. It's time to launch into the deep. You are ready. LISTEN.

I'm praying for you.

Today's Prayer

This morning I could feel my anxiety. I started to run down the list of things in my head that were causing anxiety. Today's meeting, tomorrow's funeral, loved ones sick...I could feel my anxiety rising. In my head I said, "I need to pray," but my head kept running down the list. I said, "Ok I need to calm down." I took a deep breath and started to think of the negative "what ifs" associated with the list. I tried to "think a prayer" but my holy thoughts were jumbled into my anxious thoughts. I needed to speak God's word to interrupt this process.

When I am afraid, I put my trust in you. (Psalm 56:3 NIV)

I kept repeating it aloud until what I was speaking was the only thing I was thinking. Then I was able to flow in prayer.

I am sharing this because God needs you to know that no one is immune to worry or anxiety. We just have to DO what God has instructed when it begins to rise. I got a lot of learning and a lot of burning...but I STILL know that the only offensive weapon I have in my armor is the sword of the spirit, which is the Word of God (Ephesians 6:17). My prayer for you today is that you will use your weapon! Open your bible, open your app...Chile open up Google and search for what you need for your situation. God's Word has power. Read it. Pray it. Speak it. God will do what God said.

I'm praying for us.

Today's Prayer

I hear this with urgency: *What is being shown is a false representation of what God is about to send. This is not from God.*

This morning I am praying for someone who is opening a door that doesn't need to be opened. The Spirit is saying your guard was up for a reason. Your discernment was right in the beginning. Don't ignore that sinking feeling in the pit of your stomach. Whether it's a business relationship, friendship, potential relationship ~ Stop and Listen again. Don't write off what you felt at first. Don't ignore red flags.

God, I bind unrighteous agreements right now in the name of Jesus. God, I pray that you send your angels in abundance to lead, guide and protect them in the name of Jesus. God be a hedge of protection for them throughout this day and help them to tune into Your voice for crucial instructions. In the name and authority of Jesus and by the power of His shed blood, I ask that you shut any doors that need to be shut in the spirit and in the natural. I pray for swift action and an absolute end to the plans of the enemy in the name of Jesus! Protect their minds and their movement from wayward thoughts and align them with Your truth. I pray this prayer by faith and in accordance with Your will and Your plan for our lives.

In Jesus' name, Amen.

Today's Prayer

Be on your guard; stand firm in the faith; be courageous; be strong. Do everything in love. (1 Corinthians 6:13-14 NIV)

These words were written by Paul as he closed one of his letters to the Church of Corinth. I pray that you will receive these instructions as God's plan for us to STAY THE COURSE!

Be on your guard ~ Watch and pray. Don't fall for empty promises that give a false sense of security.

Stand firm in the faith ~ Don't let what you see around you shake what God has placed in you.

Be courageous; be strong ~ Courage is not the absence of fear. Courage is doing it afraid.

Do everything in love ~ Love God. Love People. MORE.

I'm praying for you.

Today's Prayer

I just feel like thanking God this morning. I feel like personal victories *(yours and mine)* are close so I just want to thank God in advance! God, I thank You this morning for answered prayers. I thank You for coming through. I thank You for showing up and showing out. I thank You for keeping Your word and Your promises. I thank You that what the enemy meant for bad You turned it around for my good.

Thank You for looking beyond my faults and seeing my needs. Thank You for turning my stumble into a run. Thank You for turning my detour into a short cut. I thank You that the weapons didn't prosper. God, I thank You that some of the weapons didn't even form! You O God are worthy of all the praise, honor and glory! And today I will make time to THANK YOU!

In Jesus' name, Hallelujah and Amen.

Today's Prayer

God has so much in store for you. If you could just stop "waiting on the other shoe to drop." If you could stop sabotaging the good in your life because you are waiting on something to go wrong. If you could start living for God's PROMISE instead of waiting on God's punishment. One day you trust that God can do it. The next day you only trust that you are going to mess it up again. You are repeating a cycle of making money and losing money. Making progress but never finishing. Jumping in great relationships and jumping out before you get hurt ~ not even realizing that you get hurt every time you jump. One step forward. Two steps back.

And still...God has so much in store for you. My prayer for you is that you will discover why you believe God will only bless you to a certain extent. My prayer is that you will discover why you decide how long you can be happy and then undermine your own efforts. I hear it when you talk. I see it when you post. You trust God to move for others more than you trust God to move for you. I feel like I'm rambling ~ but I need you to SEE YOU. I can "shout you" all day and nothing will change in your life until you SEE YOU. Until you see the detrimental thought process that truncates your blessings and delays your destiny.

If you need a bible verse, here you go: *Be ye transformed by the renewing of your mind.* (Romans 12:2 KJV) God has so much in store for you.

I'm praying for you.

Today's Prayer

This is the day that the Lord has made. Let us rejoice and be glad in it!
(Psalm 118:24 NKJV)

God, I thank you for being the same good God for me as you have been for others. God, I thank you that I feel the prayers of the righteous. God, I rejoice because you are restoring my soul. Thank you, God, that you STILL renew the strength of the ones who wait on you. We bless your name, God! Thank you for hiding us in times of trouble. Thank you, O God, for being our refuge and strong tower. Thank you for being a resting place and then releasing us again to run and not get weary and to walk and not faint. I speak joy in sorrow. I speak hope for tomorrow. I speak beauty for ashes.

God, I bless you for a garment of praise that literally chased away a spirit of heaviness. And if you did it for me, I know you can do it for my friend reading this right now. Send your power to refill and refuel them. Send your power to encourage their hearts as they go through their own situations. I speak miracles, blessings and breakthroughs in the name of Jesus. I speak that the testimonies of God's goodness are about overflow! God, we bless you! God, we love you! God, we extol you! God, we exalt you! We give you all praise, honor and glory! In the mighty name of Jesus, we pray.

Hallelujah and Amen! Now give God GLORY!!!!

Today's Prayer

God is changing you. God is shifting your thoughts and ideas. God is widening your reach by narrowing your focus. I pray God gives you a way to mentally release and physically remove yourself from spaces that don't support or celebrate who you are becoming. It feels weird. Sometimes it feels like you are abandoning the people/places you promised you would never leave.

This is what you prayed for. Don't give up in the process. Allow God to order your steps and you will bump into your next blessing. Keep BECOMING.

I love you and I'm praying for you.

Today's Prayer

This is a declaration. Read it aloud.

Thank You, God, for allowing me to see another day. Thank You for the ups and the downs of the week. Thank You for blessing me in the ups and carrying me through the downs.

God, I thank You for walking with me. God, I thank You for fighting for me. Thank You for sending Your angels to war on my behalf.

Thank You for the new mercies of the morning. Thank You for Your grace and mercy that will cover me today.

I speak something great will happen FOR me today. I pray in expectation that a problem will be solved and a prayer will be answered. No good thing will be withheld from me today. I speak good news, open doors, prosperous opportunities and divine appointments.

Today I will feel the peace of Your presence and the power of Your hand as You work things out for my good. God, I thank You in advance for a joyful and productive day.

It is so, in the matchless name of Jesus. Amen and Amen.

Today's Prayer

I have a few friends who are experiencing sickness right now. This is the word God dropped in my spirit for them:

And after you have suffered a little while, the God of all grace, who has called you to his eternal glory in Christ, will himself restore, confirm, strengthen, and establish you. (1 Peter 5:10 ESV)

The GRACE in this Scripture is that the suffering is only for a "little while." And for that, I give God praise. But the SHOUT in this Scripture is tucked near the end. See, I often pray that God sends angels to comfort or to fight on our behalf. This Scripture says, "WILL HIMSELF" *(go read it again)*. God Himself is going to show up! God will Himself RESTORE. God will Himself CONFIRM. God will Himself STRENGTHEN. God will Himself ESTABLISH. God is going to show up in the suffering.

I decree and declare this for my friends and family, and I speak it for yours. It is so! In the name of the One who keeps showing up for us. His name is Jesus.

I'm praying for you.

Today's Prayer

Look for the good. That's what I kept hearing in prayer this morning. Look for the good. We spend the majority of our time focused on what we don't have. We spend the majority of our time IN PRAYER focusing on what we need or on what is going wrong. Yet, even as things are going wrong all around us ~ God is STILL doing good stuff. I pray that today you will look for the good.

I pray that today you will see God's hand of provision on your life. I pray today you will acknowledge the presence and protection of the Almighty God. I pray today that you will reflect and respect how God is showing up for you in this season.

I decree and declare that you will renew your mind to the goodness of God. GOD is already good. God is ALREADY good. God is already GOOD!

All day today: Look for the good. When you see it, give God a good praise...and watch your atmosphere shift.

I'm praying for you.

Today's Prayer

If you read this and think of someone or if you read this and feel "a certain kind of way" ~ God is talking to you. Respond accordingly. Get help if you need it. I love y'all for real.

It is time to walk in forgiveness. You must stop moving on from situations and circumstances and never dealing with the HARD issues and the HEART issues. You are carrying your past pain and hurt like a badge of honor. You "brag" about how you made it through what they did. But are you really "through" it? Are you really through WITH it?

You have made yourself the hero of the story when you tell it ~ and you tell it often. Yet you still have emotions that come to the surface when you talk about it or things happen that trigger old memories... and the sadness and hurt feels like it just happened yesterday. Your guard is still up and your level of tolerance for the mistakes of others is still down. It takes courage and maturity to forgive. Forgiveness is not about setting "them" free ~ it is about setting YOU free.

Forgive them. Forgive yourself.

Life is short.

It's time to walk in forgiveness.

Today's Prayer

Romans 12:12

(NIV) *Be joyful in hope, patient in affliction, faithful in prayer.*

(NLT) *Rejoice in our confident hope. Be patient in trouble and keep on praying.*

PATIENCE: the capacity to accept or tolerate delay, trouble, or suffering without getting angry or upset.

Today, I speak a confident hope over you. Confident because you have seen God show up. Confident because you have receipts from God working things out in your life. Your hope is no longer based on what you were told as a child. God has proven God's self to you time and time again. Because of this confident hope, we can be joyful. We can rejoice because we know the track record of the God we serve. Whatever you are waiting on, whatever you have been praying and crying about, I pray that God will release joy as you put your hope in Him.

I decree according to the Word of God that you will have the capacity to wait patiently. Delays won't break you. Trouble won't shake you. I bind anger or any emotion that will cause you to move too quickly and act outside of God's intended will for your life. I release a praying spirit in every situation. As you wait- keep on praying. As you hope ~ keep on praying. The prayers of the righteous are powerful and effective. Keep on praying. The One who promised is faithful.

In Jesus' name, Amen.

Today's Prayer

Praying for the ones who have to be silent. The ones who cannot share what happened or what's happening. The ones who have to be strong because life as they know it would fall apart if they shared what was inside. The husband who feels his wife wouldn't understand. The mother who can't share because she doesn't want the children scared. I'm praying for you. The Pastor who feels she/he has to keep up appearances but who is frustrated with God's plan. The one in the relationship that everyone thinks is amazing but the secrets and the settling are becoming more than you can bear.

I'm praying for you. The single one. The married one. The gay one. The depressed one. The forgotten one. The heartbroken one. The pissed off one. Whichever "one" YOU are. Please know that the ONE who sees all ~ SEES YOU. Jesus Christ, the Sovereign One, hears your silent scream.

I love you and I am praying for you.

Today's Prayer

God, we trust You. Keep us in perfect peace as we keep our minds on You. If our thoughts drift to things that are unsettling and begin to drain us, I speak that we will be reminded to cast our cares on God because God cares for us. I speak that we will be reminded that God's peace guards our hearts and minds in Christ Jesus. I speak that we will be overcome with peace when we are reminded that greater is He that is IN US than he that is in the world!

God, we stand on Your Word that says those who plant seeds of peace will reap a harvest of righteousness. Saturate our walk, our talk our hearts and our homes with a divine peace that only our Creator can give. When we rise, PEACE! When we rest, PEACE! When we go out, PEACE! When we come in, PEACE! We decree it. We declare it. We call it forth in the Spirit. Manifest Your PEACE O God! And we will be careful to give You all glory, honor and praise. It is so!

In Jesus' name, Amen.

Today's Prayer

Sometimes I feel like I'm nowhere near my goals and plans. Sometimes I feel like I'm floating along with no "real" strategy. Sometimes I feel like I look good on paper but not really sure of how it will all come together. Then God speaks. Then God shows up. Then God removes the barrier. Then God releases a blessing. Then God commands a breakthrough. Then it all makes sense.

I pray today that however you feel about yourself and your progress ~ that God will show you how God feels. I pray that God will show up today and make your VISION and your VICTORY clear. I speak barriers removed and blessings released. I touch and agree with your prayers that are in alignment with God's Word.

I speak that God will command a breakthrough in your circumstances in the name of Jesus! God is not the author of confusion so I speak clarity in your decision making. God has not abandoned you in your storm so I speak comfort and peace to your spirit. God will not stop loving you. God has not changed God's mind about you. God's plans for you are still in full effect. Get out of your head and into God's will. I promise the safest place in the whole wide world is in the will of God.

I'm praying for you.

Today's Prayer

I pray that today in your quiet time you experience a moment of truth that breaks down your walls of anxiety and allows you to come face to face and heart to heart with the love of God. I pray that you can find sacred space to be open and honest about the places in your spirit that are overloaded and also the places that are empty.

In that space of transparency, I speak transformation in the name of Jesus. In that sacred space, I pray you see God. In that sacred space, I pray you see YOU. I pray you see that you have taken on too much. I pray you see that you have given your all. I pray you see that you are doing your best.

May the Lord our God ease your burdens, lift your spirit, and fill every empty place with peace...until it overflows. Make some time to meet with Jesus today. I think He would love to talk to you.

I'm praying for you.

Today's Prayer

I need thee, O, I need thee;
every hour I need thee;
O bless me now, my Savior
I come to thee.
~I Need Thee Every Hour (Annie Hawks 1872)

God, we need Your grace. God, we need Your mercy. God, we need Your provision. God, we need Your protection. God, we need Your healing. God, we need Your HELP! We come to You for the blessings that only You can provide. Bless us now Savior! Bless our finances now God. Bless students and teachers now God. Bless healthcare workers now God. Bless those without power now God. Bless the unemployed now God. Bless the overworked now God. Bless those who are suffering with all manners of diseases now God. Your Word says that we should approach God's throne of grace with confidence, so that we may receive mercy and find grace to help us in our time of need.

Here we are, God. Confident that You alone are able.

Help us.

We need You.

We pray this prayer in the name of the One who Saves.

His name is Jesus. Amen and Amen.

Today's Prayer

God, I still can't believe ALL the ways that You've made! Thank you for making a way when I didn't trust You. Thank you for making a way when I didn't put you first. Thank you for making a way OUT of what I got myself IN. Thank you for making a way over! Thank you for making a way through! God is incredible! God deserves an incredible praise!

When your heart is heavy, and you are facing things that you can't control ~ remember the One who is in control. Remember the One who is a WAYMAKER! Begin to list the times God made a way for YOU! And if God did it before ~ God can do it AGAIN! God is incredible! God deserves an incredible praise!

Today's Prayer

Praying for the one who has been at the end of their rope for a long time. It has felt like God has forgotten and left you in misery. God is about to lift you out of the miry* clay and set you on a solid foundation where every step will be secure. God never forgot. God has literally sustained you at the end of your rope. God sustained your hope until it was time for a change. It's time. God has seen you praying for others, wishing others well in their success. The same is about to happen for you. Because you prayed for others, because you did not succumb to jealous and envious thoughts, God is sending your ram in the bush! You will NOT have to sacrifice what you love. Jehovah-Jireh[1] is here! Receive your breakthrough in the name of Jesus.

I'm praying for you.

Scripture References:

I waited patiently for the Lord; And He inclined to me, And heard my cry. He also brought me up out of a horrible pit, Out of the miry* clay, And set my feet upon a rock, And established my steps.
(Psalm 40:1-2 NIV)
*miry comes from the word mire> thick mud; troublesome situation...

Abraham looked up and there in a thicket he saw a ram caught by its horns. He went over and took the ram and sacrificed it as a burnt offering instead of his son. So Abraham called that place The Lord Will Provide. And to this day it is said, "On the mountain of the Lord it will be provided."
(Genesis 22:13-14 NIV)

[1]Jehovah Jireh ~ God our Provider

Today's Prayer

There is something stirring in your spirit and you can't let it go. You can no longer ignore it or attempt to cover it up with how busy you already are. Now is the time to HONOR the desire that God has placed in you to use your gifts to be a blessing to others. This is how it starts. This is how your next chapter starts. See, you want to know God's FINAL plan for you ~ but if you could see the ultimate plan ~ you would decide that you weren't equipped for it and you would discourage yourself.

So, God is only showing you the next step. And trust me...You have everything you need to take the next step. Outline the book. Buy the domain name. Download the 501c3 paperwork. Introduce the new product. Use your phone for the video and stop waiting on the expensive camera. Fill out the application. Write the resignation letter.

The burning will not go away. God knows the plans God has for you and they are NOT to give up on you. God will not give up. God will not turn away. God will not leave you alone. Take a deep breath and do what it takes to start your next chapter. And I am sure of this: He who has begun a good work in you will continue to complete it.

I'm praying for you.

Today's Prayer

Whatever I face today this will be my phrase: *Work it Out Lord!*

God help us to hand our issues and concerns over to you. Remind us, according to the wisdom you gave our ancestors, that while we are trying to figure it out ~ You have already worked it out. We surrender to Your will. We take our hands off now. We will get out of your way. Help us to STAY out of Your business! Work it out, Lord. I speak that when we say these words today You will release peace that will surpass our understanding. In that moment of peace, we will know without a doubt that You O God have shown up in our situation and everything will be alright.

We love you.

We trust you.

Work it out, Lord!

It is so. In Jesus' name, Amen.

Today's Prayer

God release your strength to Your people. Release your endurance, God. Release your perseverance God! Release Your joy ~ let it fall like rain! For every person who feels like their back is against the wall. For every person who feels stuck between a rock and a hard place ~ I speak the Word of God over your life. The power of God over your situation. Satan the Lord God rebuke thee! Take your hands off the people of God. I bind the assignments of the enemy for fear, chaos and confusion. I loose the peace of God in the name of Jesus. I loose the spirit of healing in the name of Jesus.

God, we see the weapon that has formed. God, we feel the weapon that has formed. God, we speak with power and the assurance of the Holy Spirit that the weapon may form but it will not prosper! The weapon may form but it will not prosper! The weapon may form but it WILL NOT PROSPER! We speak a prospering of Your Word. A prospering of Your purpose. A prospering of Your divine plans. A prospering of blessings. A prospering of breakthroughs in the name of Jesus.

I decree and declare according to God's word that you will prosper in all things and be in good health ~ even as your soul prospers. I call it to be so ~ In the name and authority of Jesus and by the power of His shed blood.

Hallelujah and Amen!

Today's Prayer

No matter what happens around me today, O God, You are the center of my joy. My hope is in Your Word. My peace is in Your promise. My protection is in Your power. You said You would strengthen me. You said You would help me. You said You would uphold me with your righteous right hand.

God, I believe what You said because I saw what You did! I saw you make a way for me when I couldn't see a way out. I saw You open doors for me when I didn't deserve it. I saw You answer my prayers after I thought You had forgotten about me. Trouble can't make me doubt you 'cause I know too much about you!

I will wait on You! I know You will show up. I know You will answer. I know You will work it together for good. My HOPE is in Your Word. My PEACE is in Your promise. My PROTECTION is in Your power.

And it IS so! In the matchless name of Jesus. Amen and Amen.

Today's Prayer

These are crazy times. It is so easy to get caught up in the downward spiral of fear and negativity. Today, I pray that we will not be conformed to the fear of the world but that we will be transformed by the renewing of our minds. Lord, help us to stop waiting on the other shoe to drop. Help us to be fully present when good things happen and not fret about what is coming next. Help us to be cautious but not fearful; Careful but not anxious. God, Your Word encourages us not to worry ~ help us to cling to Your Word. Help us to let not our hearts be troubled. We believe in You. We believe what You promised. Now God, help our unbelief.

Today, we will make every effort to take our negative thoughts captive and speak only that which is fruitful and prosperous in the atmosphere. According to Philippians 4:8, we will fix our thoughts on what is true, and honorable, and right, and pure, and lovely, and admirable; only thinking about things that are excellent and worthy of praise. Protect our peace, God. Protect our joy. And we will be careful to give you all of the praise, honor, and glory.

In Jesus' name, Amen.

Today's Prayer

There is a specific calling on your life. You've gotten glimpses but not a full picture. God desires to use you for more than what you can see. God's plan for you includes accomplishments that are beyond your current capacity. You haven't answered the call because you don't feel ready. REMEMBER: God doesn't always call the equipped, but God will equip the called. Stop hiding in the safety of what you know. It's time to meet God in the unchartered territory. You keep trying to figure it out, label it and make it match your level of comfort.

This move will be uncomfortable because you need to UNLEARN some unproductive faith habits. You're so programmed to "name it, claim it and shout the victory" that you are missing lessons and stunting your growth. Growth happens in the process not in the promise. Answer the call. Be uncomfortable. Your destiny is waiting.

I'm praying for you.

Today's Prayer

Here is another Scripture I pray for those who are struggling with their faith as they face difficult times. Praying it lately for those who are dealing with COVID ~ whether they are the patient or the caregiver or a loved one:

So do not throw away your confidence; it will be richly rewarded. You need to persevere so that when you have done the will of God, you will receive what he has promised. For, in just a little while, he who is coming will come and will not delay. (Hebrews 10:35-37 NIV)

Don't stop believing. There is a confidence that you've had in the past as it related to your faith ~ especially when things were going well. Tap into THAT confidence. Your reward is attached to that confidence. God's response is attached to your faith. You NEED to PERSEVERE! God's promise is attached to your perseverance.

And here's the promise: In just a little while, God is coming. God WILL come and God will not delay. When God shows up ~ healing shows up! When God shows up ~ peace shows up! When God shows up ~ deliverance shows up! In a little while, God will come, and God will not delay.

I'm praying for you.

Today's Prayer

This is the day that the Lord has made; let us rejoice and be glad in it. (Psalm 118:24 NRSV)

God, we thank You for allowing us to see another day. We rejoice because You didn't have to do it ~ but You did! We rejoice because with everything going on in the world...today, we were still on the wake-up list. We rejoice because every time we see another day. There is hope for You to change our circumstance, shift our situation and prepare us for Your purpose. Today we will rejoice. Today we will be glad.

Thank You God for another day to serve You. Thank You God for another day to love You. Thank You God for another chance to get it right! You are AMAZING GOD! We love You. We honor You. We bless Your Holy Name! We offer this prayer and this praise in the name of the One who died for us to have another chance. His name is Jesus.

Amen and Amen.

Dr. Karren D. Todd

Today's Prayer

I believe in praying God's word. This is one of the Scriptures that I pray over those who are dealing with COVID or any dire sickness. I included a sample prayer but honestly, my prayer is different every time I read it. Feel free to pray your own. Use the Scripture as a foundation and let us stand in faith and petition on behalf of our friends and family.

Then they cried to the Lord in their trouble, and he saved them from their distress. He sent out his word and healed them; he rescued them from the grave. (Psalm 107:19-20 NIV)

God, I am so grateful that we can come to You when we are in trouble. As we come to You, we honor who You are as our Creator and our Healer. Our crying out to You honors who You are as our Provider and our Protector. God, our coming to You proves our faith in Your word that says You will hear and answer. It shows forth our faith in Your word that says when we ~ Your people ~ cry out. You will save us from our distress. Save us O God!

Today, I am specifically praying for _____. Save them from the pain. Save them from the shortness of breath. Save them from mental anguish. Save them from loneliness. According to your word, I decree and declare that You will send Your word and heal them; You will rescue them from the grave. I speak that this sickness is NOT unto death in the name of Jesus! I know that You have all power and authority to speak, heal and rescue. We've seen You do it. Do it again for _____. We stand on Your Word and we pray it by faith. Speak God! Heal God! Rescue God! It is so, in the name of Jesus.

Amen and Amen.

Today's Prayer

You are spending too much time and energy focusing on what was. Attempting to recreate what God has removed. History and accomplishments have their place and their purpose, but most of those things are now devoid of power. God's power is active. We serve the one true and living God. Don't miss what God IS doing and IS promising to do because you are still trying to hold on to yesterday's press clippings or eat yesterday's manna. Many of the things we are yearning for weren't even working for us. We were already praying for something different. Yet now we are longing for our past dysfunction.

God help us to look forward. God help us to lean into the new season with faith and gratitude. God help us to focus on what is and what is to come. God help us to survive the discomfort of losing what was so that YOU can birth a better version of us, a better version of the church and a better version of our world. We love you, God. Help us to trust your plan.

In Jesus' name, Amen.

Today's Prayer

Today God will show you God's kindness and compassion. Grace and mercy will surround you and follow you throughout your day. Anxiety will not overtake you. The peace of God will guard your heart and your mind through Christ Jesus. Be of good courage today and God will strengthen your heart. Divine wisdom and discernment will be yours. Decisions will be easier because of the clarity God is giving you right now. The joy of the Lord will cover you and the favor of God will keep you.

Today God's angels of protection will war on your behalf. Today the weapons may form, but they will not prosper. The things that will prosper today are your health and your soul. I speak healing to your body, your mind and your spirit. Today is your "another chance." Face today like God is with you ~ because God is.

I love you and I'm praying for you.

Dr. Karren D. Todd

Today's Prayer

I keep hearing: DISCIPLINE. We are not going back to what used to be so it's time to figure out how to be disciplined in this version of life. There are areas of life that you are neglecting and it's keeping you from moving forward. Your lack of discipline is blocking the path to your next open door. There are some things you do like clockwork and others that can't seem to make it off your to do list... and the anxiety of this pandemic has made it worse. Lack of discipline feels calm and relaxing. It feels like you are taking a deep breath and letting your hair down. Lack of discipline is the whole bag of chips, the extra items in the cart, the risky get together with friends.

I need you to acknowledge that lack of discipline feels good in the moment but the consequences are keeping you stagnant. You are creating your own setbacks and praying like God won't deliver you. Walk in discipline and deliver yourself. If you want your life to shift ~ shift your discipline.

Discipline has nothing to do with what you think you deserve. Discipline is sacrifice. Yet, it is discipline that produces the harvest. Let's apply some of this "wake up and check FB" discipline to the "write a chapter in your book" discipline or "do some crunches" discipline. Oh, if you need a Scripture, read Hebrews 12:11 and know that I am praying for US!

No discipline seems pleasant at the time, but painful. Later on, however, it produces a harvest of righteousness and peace for those who have been trained by it. (NIV)

Today's Prayer

This is what I heard in my spirit around 4am: *If you START NOW, God will grant SUPERNATURAL movement that will allow you to REDEEM THE TIME you wasted in fear and procrastination.*

This is my prayer for us to receive that word.

God we receive the promise of supernatural movement in the name of Jesus! We confess that we haven't done all that You have asked. We confess that we have allowed fear and procrastination to slow us down and even convince us that what You promised may never happen for us. We confess that we have tried to change the meaning of what You said to something that was less challenging and more comfortable for us. We confess our doubt in Your plan. We confess our disregard for Your timing. We confess that we have been hearers and thinkers and "pray"ers and note-takers and advice givers and planners, but we have NOT been DOERS. We confess and we ask for Your forgiveness.

Thank You for forgiving us and giving us another chance to START NOW. Thank You for the promise to redeem our time. Thank You that our fear and our procrastination have not disqualified us from Your promise. We will start now. We will begin today. We will pick up the instructions and become the DOERS that You have called us to be. Now God we stand ready for You to finish the work that You have begun in and through us.

It is so.

In Jesus' name, Amen.

Today's Prayer

Get back on track. I don't know where you were heading or where God was guiding you, but you have let your circumstances alter your ambitions. Whatever happened was supposed to strengthen you... redirect you ~ it was not sent to stop you. You got scared or frustrated or your feelings got hurt and you just...stopped. It's time to get back on track.

This week I pray God increases your DETERMINATION. I pray God sends a WIN that increases your CONFIDENCE. I pray that God will show you a sign that He is still WITH you. I pray that doors that were once closed will be taken off the hinges never to be closed again. I pray that God would even answer a prayer that you've stopped praying! I speak a breakthrough in your life that destroys that yoke of complacency that has caused you to settle for less than God's will for your life.

I bind those negative, discouraging thoughts and release flames of hope that burn up any seeds of doubt the enemy has planted in your mind. I speak a divine awakening in the name of Jesus! Breathe life back into their dreams, O God. Revive the hope that they can accomplish anything with You. Restore the fire that once had them running toward their goals. Redeem the time that was lost in fear and complacency. You can STILL have what God promises. You can STILL have what you heard God say. You can STILL achieve what God showed you. Shake the dust from your feet and get back on track!

I'm praying for you.

Weekly Prayers

Just as prayer sets the spiritual pace for your day, I also believe in speaking blessings and breakthroughs over the upcoming week. These weekly prayers will prepare your mind and spirit to set your expectations for the week as well as embrace whatever life brings. Pray them. Meditate on them. I pray you receive God's grace and God's power each time you are intentional to start your week in God's presence.

This Week's Prayer

As we begin this week, I speak protection and provision in the name of Jesus. God when it feels like trouble is all around us and the enemy is coming in like a flood ~ I speak according to Your word that You will send the Holy Spirit to raise a standard against him. Raise the standard O God! Be our hedge of protection. Protect us on the right and on the left. Be our rearguard and go before us in the name of Jesus. By the divine power that works in us, we cancel every plot, plan, scheme and trick of the enemy. We decree and declare according to Your word that no weapon formed against us shall prosper. That every tongue and every word that rises against us in judgment ~ YOU shall condemn.

This week God's promises WILL be fulfilled in our lives. God's word will be powerful and effective in our lives. This week we will walk in the favor of God. This week we will dwell in the peace of God. This week we will experience the power of God working things out for our good. We will start fresh. We will finish what we start. We speak it and it IS so!

In the matchless name of Jesus Christ ~ Hallelujah and Amen!

This Week's Prayer

This morning I pray for a positive and productive week for you. I speak good decisions that benefit your future and your finances. I speak good connections that accelerate God's plan for you. I bind small thinking and thoughts of defeat. I loose a mindset of purpose and victory. You WILL have what God promised. Negative people will not have the power to guilt you out of God's grace. I speak that God will enlarge your territory this week in the name of Jesus! As you align with the will of God, you will see the goodness of the Lord.

I decree and declare that this week you will not have to fight for your peace and you will not struggle to find joy. I speak there is a YES in the atmosphere. As God says yes to you, I pray you will say yes to God. Say YES to the blessing! Say YES to the breakthrough! Peace. Joy. Favor. Victory. YES! They all belong to you. And It is so! In Jesus' name.

Have an amazing week!

This Week's Prayer

A prayer of expectation for the week.

[Read Aloud] *God, I thank you in advance for a good and productive week. This week I decree and declare that the God who is OVER all, THROUGH all, and IN all is working on my behalf. All that I have been trying to figure out on my own, God has already worked out in my favor. I speak that I will have patience in the process as God fulfills every promise. This week I will see God's grace in situations that I had given up on.*

Blessings will manifest this week. Provision will manifest this week. Resources will manifest this week. Healing will manifest this week. I speak it and it IS so! I pray that my anxiety level is low and my peace level is high. I speak that my fear will decrease and my faith will increase. I pray that I will have more ups than downs ~ More joy than sorrow ~ More hope than heartache ~ More smiles than tears. I anticipate good news this week. I look forward to good news this week. I expect good news this week. I ask and receive it all in the name of Jesus.

Amen and Amen.

This Week's Prayer

Praying peace and favor for your week. I pray that your anxiety level stays low and your gratitude level stays high. I pray that you are able to handle disappointment with grace and any offenses with mercy. I speak that you will find joy in the smallest things and humility is your greatest achievement.

My hope is that you will surround yourself with people that celebrate and elevate you mentally and spiritually. And as you pray for others, cheer for others, forgive others, love others ~ I pray that God will do the same for you.

This Week's Prayer

As I pray for this upcoming week, I pray that God will grant you complete knowledge of His will for this season of your life. I speak spiritual wisdom and understanding in your decision making. I pray that you will hear God's voice clearly, recognize that it is God and act accordingly. I speak that you will see the path before you and have the courage to allow God to order your steps. I bind doubt and delay and ask God to increase your faith to HEAR and OBEY.

I come against the internal panic and stress that this crisis is causing and I decree and declare that this week you will experience God's PEACE in your process, God's STRENGTH in your weakness and God's FAVOR in your finances. I speak a divine return on investments this week and I decree according to God's word that God will release good fruit from the seeds you have sown.

Blessings and Breakthroughs!
Blessings and Breakthroughs!
Blessings and Breakthroughs!
In the mighty name of Jesus, I pray ~ Hallelujah and Amen!

Have an amazing week and know that even when you can't find the words ~ someone is praying for you.

This Week's Prayer

It's time to PUSH! I pray that this is the week you will birth what you have been carrying in your heart and in your spirit. I speak that the labor pains you have been feeling will bring forth the NEW THING you have been praying for. I pray that this is the week you can push your dream into reality. I speak this will be the week that your visions will produce victory in the name of Jesus!

Push through anxiety. Push through fear. Push through negativity. Push beyond who you used to be and walk into the season of who you are becoming. P.U.S.H.! PRAY Until Something Happens! PRAISE Until Something Happens! God is going to do what God promised.

I'm praying for you and it's time for you to PUSH!!

This Week's Prayer

This morning I felt drained. I didn't want to move...still don't. I wanted to stay in bed all day so that my mind can recover from all of the things that my eyes have seen, my ears have heard and my heart has felt. But in the midst of all of this ~ there is still life to be lived. We still have to live. We still have to make decisions about every aspect of life. But some of those decisions that used to be second nature are now being second-guessed. And it's because we are exhausted. That little 10lb weight gets real heavy after the 3rd go 'round...So this week God, as we press through, and fight those things that are unimaginable ~ I pray that you would just GIVE US some victories this week. I don't want to be out of order ~ but God I've seen you do that in my life. I ask that you HELP us with some of this stuff...and then just HAND us some of this other stuff.

God, don't let the enemy weigh us down and get small wins because we are drained. I speak SWEAT-LESS victories in this season in the name of Jesus! Favor us O God! Restore our joy. Renew our spirits. Rebuild our faith. Revive our hearts. Revive us AGAIN O God! Thank you in advance for VICTORY! Victory today! Victory this week! We speak it and call it to be so according to Your Word. We rejoice right now because we know that we offer this prayer in the name of the One who WON IT ALL on a hill called Calvary! His name is Jesus.

Hallelujah and Amen!

This Week's Prayer

As we pray for a productive and blessed week, I speak the instructions of Romans 12:12 (NKJV) over your life ~ that you will *"rejoice in hope, be patient in tribulation, [and] be constant in prayer."* While you live out these divine instructions, I pray that you will have the work ethic of Noah, the spiritual discipline of Daniel, and the faith of Abraham.

I speak that God will gird you with the DISCERNMENT and WISDOM of Deborah; PERSEVERANCE in prayer like Hannah and even the COURAGE of Esther for such a time as this. I decree an acceleration of blessings and breakthroughs according to your faith and the purposed plan of God. I pray this prayer in the peace and power of the name of Jesus. It is so.

Amen and Amen.

This Week's Prayer

Praying for your strength to do the hard thing this week. The conversation that you have been avoiding, the work you have been ignoring, the situation you have been delaying...it is time. I bind fear and release courage in the name of Jesus. I speak determination and a mental toughness that will allow you to focus and not waver. God give them the words to say and the steps to take to address this matter. If it involves people, God, I pray that you would minimize any fallout or backlash.

God, shield and protect your children as we do what is right and what is righteous. I decree that there will be a RELEASE and there will be RELIEF when it is accomplished. Your blessing is on the other side of this. Your breakthrough is attached to the outcome. It has to be done. No more delays.

I'm praying for you.

This Week's Prayer

Whatever you are facing this week ~ there is still hope. The hope may not look like you want it to look, but it is there. Hope exists as long as you do. Hope exists as long as God exists. I pray that you won't allow your circumstances or the circumstances of the world to take away your hope. God is a God of Hope. I speak that you will receive Paul's instructions to rejoice in hope. I speak that you will walk in your faith which is the assurance and the substance of things hoped for. I speak that you will tap into God's plan for you that promises a hope and a future.

I decree and declare, according to God's word, that your hope will not disappoint. Your hope will not put you to shame. Your hope will produce confidence. Your hope will strengthen your prayers. Your hope will set up your breakthrough. I speak a hope that brings forth God's favor. I speak a hope that fully supports God's guarantee. I speak a hope that demands a praise BEFORE the promise. A hope that says, "Don't wait 'til the battle is over! Shout Now!" I speak HOPE and call it to be so in the powerful name of Jesus.

Hallelujah and Amen!

This Week's Prayer

Hebrews 12:1

Therefore, since we are surrounded by such a great cloud of witnesses, let us throw off everything that hinders and the sin that so easily entangles. And let us run with perseverance the race marked out for us, (NIV)

...let us strip off every weight that slows us down, especially the sin that so easily trips us up. And let us run with endurance the race God has set before us. (NLT)

This Week's Prayer

Psalm 90:17

May the favor of the Lord our God rest on us; establish the work of our hands for us— yes, establish the work of our hands. (NIV)

And may the Lord our God show us his approval and make our efforts successful. (NLT)

Yes, make our efforts successful! I pray that this week God's unmerited favor will rest on you. I pray that you will have multiple options for the things you have been praying for. Doors will open and possibilities will manifest. People will call with opportunities because someone mentioned your name to them. I speak that God will show God's approval in spiritual and tangible ways. I pray that God will establish your efforts and MAKE them successful.

For those who didn't see how they would make it through, out, or over—I speak options on top of options! God's favor multiplied in the name of Jesus! I pray that because God has already approved ~ there is no wrong answer. As long as you give God glory, God will make what you choose successful. You have struggled with this long enough. God says rest in the divine favor that is waiting for you. I speak it and it IS so! In the mighty and matchless name of Jesus.

Hallelujah and Amen.

This Week's Prayer

I pray that God does something this week to blow your mind! I pray that God answers a prayer you forgot you prayed. I pray that God opens a door that you didn't even know you had access to. I pray that you get news so good that it takes your breath and leaves you speechless. God still has the whole world in His hands. God is still showing up. God is still doing good stuff. God is still working miracles.

I pray God blows up your spot this week just to let you know that the King of Glory is still on the throne! This is my prayer for you and when it happens...tag me in the testimony! Have an amazing week.

I love you for real.

This Week's Prayer

God, as we start this week, I pray for restoration. The conditions of the world have affected our outlook. The circumstances of life are weighing on our hearts. God, we have not lost our hope, but we are fighting daily to hold onto the measure that we have left. You, O God, are El Roi the God who sees. So we know that, even in this, You are watching over us.

We just ask that you restore us, in the name of Jesus. Restore the joy of our salvation. Restore the favor that You spoke over us. Restore the peace that You promised we could have access to. God, we cry out to You like David when he wrote:

Though you have made me see troubles...you will restore my life again; from the depths of the earth You will again bring me up. You will increase my honor and comfort me once more. (Psalm 71:20-21 NIV)

We have seen, felt, and experienced the troubles. Now God, restore us again! Bring us back up! Increase honor and comfort once more in the name of Jesus.

I speak restoration in the name and authority of Jesus Christ and by the power of His shed blood! Repair and renovate us in the Spirit. Return us to our rightful position in You. Rebuild our faith, God. Recondition our hearts and minds to be stayed on You and not focused on our problems. RESTORATION! I speak it and it is so! I pray this prayer in the name of the one who sacrificed His life to restore our relationship with our Creator. His name is Jesus and we give Him all glory, honor and praise.

Hallelujah and Amen!

This Week's Prayer

I pray that you have a productive week. I pray that you make decisions based on faith and not fear. I pray that you begin to recognize the things/people that give you energy and the things/people that drain your energy AND that you will have the courage to act accordingly. I pray that you will go ALL IN for your destiny this week. I pray that you walk in favor, live in peace, and stand on God's promises. I pray that you hear with clarity and speak with power. I pray that if God doesn't change the situation that has you bound ~ that God will free you IN the situation. Free you IN the lion's den! Free you IN the fiery furnace!

I pray that this is the week that you get out of your comfort zone and meet God in the unchartered territory. Get out of the boat and meet Jesus on the water.

I love you and I'm praying for you.

This Week's Prayer

God, I pray that this will be a week of restoration and order. I pray that You will restore the JOY of our salvation. I pray that You will restore the HOPE that has been lost due to the circumstances of life. I pray that You will restore the drive and motivation that has decreased because of the unknown. I pray that You will restore the finances of those who have reached the bottom of their bank accounts. God, I speak that this season won't steal the dreams of those who are clinging to Your promises. Restore us in the name of Jesus! And even as you restore God, increase our desire to do the work of restoration. God help us to set things in order according to Your instructions.

Help us to do what needs to be done and finish what needs to be finished so that we will be aligned with Your work in this season. God, we realize that faith without works is useless. So, God, give us the grace and favor to do our part. I decree according to Your word that our efforts to be in Your divine order will POSITION us for Your PROMISES!

Establish the work of our hands, God, and we will be careful to give Your name all of the glory, honor and praise. We offer this prayer in the name of the One who did the work so that we might be restored to our rightful place in God. His name is Jesus.

Hallelujah and Amen!

This Week's Prayer

This is an excerpt from *Power Walk*, a devotional journal I released in 2017. I rarely read my own stuff, but this is where I landed today as I asked God to strengthen you so that you wouldn't let frustration throw you off of God's path. I pray that this week your frustration will not exceed your faith. God is STILL in control. Keep trusting. God is going to do what God said.

Power Walk - Day 5: God is able to deliver so it frustrates us when He doesn't. However, if God always delivered you immediately, you would have no need for faith and you would never learn to trust Him. The situation you're going through is not out of control; it's just out of YOUR control. My prayer for you today is that instead of being anxious about 'when' and 'how much longer' – you find peace in knowing that He's with you right now during your valley experience. God doesn't just show up with the promise, He walks with you (or even carries you) through the process.

Keep trusting. God is going to do what He said.

Signed: A Living Witness

Even though I walk through the valley of the shadow of death, I will fear no evil, for you are with me; your rod and your staff, they comfort me.
(Psalm 23:4 NIV84)

This Week's Prayer

God is releasing opportunities. You've been praying for open doors. Don't miss what God is doing because you are watching the wrong door. The blessing is coming in a way you don't expect... because you don't know what you need in THIS season to prepare you for the unknown normal of the next season. I speak clarity of thought in the name of Jesus. I speak heightened discernment in the name of Jesus.

Pay attention THIS WEEK to what makes you feel uneasy. I decree and declare that only God's way will feel right. Only the Godsent opportunity will bring a settling in your spirit. This may not be exactly what you prayed for, but it will put you on the path to what God promised. I speak a release of positional promises in the name of Jesus! You've been praying.

God has heard you.

God is about to respond...

This Week's Prayer

God, we thank You that with every new day comes new strength, new thoughts and new mercy. In the newness of this day, we take this moment of thanksgiving to proclaim what we believe. God, we believe that You give us peace that surpasses our understanding. We believe that even in sorrow You can give us immeasurable joy. God, we believe that Your perfect love casts out fear.

Now based on what we believe, we speak in the name and the authority of Jesus Christ that today we will feel less of yesterday's pain and more of tomorrow's promise. You promised us peace. You promised us joy. You promised us love ~ and today we receive the promises of God. We decree and declare every manifested promise in the name of Jesus! So as we enter this new week, give us a peace that we cannot explain, a joy down on the inside that won't stop making us smile and a love that chases away our fear.

We speak it according to Your Word and we believe it to be so ~ in the mighty and matchless name of Jesus.

Amen and Amen.

This Week's Prayer

This week I pray that you will be open to the new thing that God is doing in your life. Be open to learning or trying something different ~ it's difficult to get to a new place driving in the same circle. This "new thing" just might be the door to what you have been praying for.

Oh, and I changed the pronouns in this prayer so that you can read it aloud and speak great things for your week.

I love y'all for real!

This Week's Prayer

God, I pray that this will be a week of PEACE. Help us to seek peace and pursue it. Help us to look for ways to be peaceful in our communication with others ~ even when we disagree. I speak peace in our homes. I speak peace in our families. God, I pray with all that is in me that You will help us to find peace with living distant and different in this season. God, I bind the fatigue and anxiety that is pushing some to be reckless and go back to the comfort of closeness. We need your peace, O God, to stay the course. In every situation we face this week, I speak a peace that transcends our understanding. I speak a divine peace that will guard our hearts.

I speak that same peace will guard our minds in the name of Jesus. God, I pray that we are so filled with peace that it will overflow in every encounter. I speak that when we enter a room or get on a virtual call that the peace of God will overflow and shift the atmosphere! This week we decree and declare a mind-changing, mood-altering peace in the name of Jesus!

Finally, God help us to pray and not worry about our government. Give us peace about all governmental affairs ~ locally and nationally. We speak our desire for a government that is truly for the people and by the people in the name of Jesus. Yet, even with that desire, help us to ground our faith in the fact that whoever is in the White House ~You, O God, are still on the throne. And God, we will forever be careful to give Your Name all the glory, honor and praise. Thank You in advance for Your presence, Your peace and Your power. We offer this prayer in the name of the One who IS peace ~ His name is Jesus.

Amen and Amen.

This Week's Prayer

Let the words of my mouth and the meditation of my heart - Be acceptable in Your sight, O Lord, my strength and my Redeemer.

(Psalm 19:14 NKJV)

God, I pray that you will align our words with your will as we keep our minds stayed on You. Help us to speak love and light this week to help lead others out of dark situations. I speak that the words we choose this week will build up and encourage others. God, we recognize that our words have power. Help us to pay attention to what we are speaking over ourselves, over our children and over all who we come in contact with this week. God even give us the wisdom and discernment to NOT speak if we don't have anything good to say.

I pray that you would fill our hearts with Your word so that when we open our mouths ~ we will speak Your promises and saturate the atmosphere with peace, hope and healing. Now God we ask, according to Your word, that You will let the words of our mouths and the meditations of our heart be acceptable in Your sight. We pray this prayer in the name of the One whose words redeem us and continue to give us strength ~ His name is Jesus.

Amen and Amen.

This Week's Prayer

The world is too heavy right now for YOU to walk around with old baggage and unaddressed issues. Take a moment to name the things/people you need to remove from your space for your SANITY. Name the habits/behaviors you need to leave alone to LEVEL UP. Name the thought processes that you need to pause for your PEACE. Stop ignoring the things, the people, the sins that keep tripping you up. It's time for you to get tired of falling.

I speak that you will no longer be hindered, entangled, slowed down or tripped up. I speak an end to you allowing yourself to be exposed to extra and unnecessary anxiety. I bind fragility and loose agility and mobility, in the name of Jesus! I pray this is the week you speak your change. I pray this is the week you make a change. I pray this is the week you believe that it IS so.

It's time to run... I'm praying for you.

This Week's Prayer

God as I enter a new week with new possibilities, I speak that I will move forward with courage because I know that You are Emmanuel ~ God with us. I speak that my faith will increase daily and I will be secure in Your promises and Your plans for me. I speak divine wisdom will guide my decisions as I do my best to become who You have destined me to be. I decree and declare that this will be a week of FAVOR! What the enemy meant for bad You, O God, are turning around for my good!

This week my joy will outweigh my sorrow and my faith will overcome my fear. I look forward to open doors and answered prayers! I stand on tiptoe in anticipation of every blessing and breakthrough that You have in store for me and my family. God, come through ~ like You always do! And I will be careful to give Your name all the glory, honor and praise.

In Jesus' name I pray, Hallelujah and Amen.

Prayers for Self-Care

Dear friend, I hope all is well with you and that you are as healthy in body as you are strong in spirit.
(3 John 1:2 NLT)

As believers we all want to be used by God. We want to make a positive impact on the lives of others. We understand sacrifice and living through difficult times. However, as you sacrifice for God's righteousness sake ~ you don't have to sacrifice caring for yourself. God desires a mentally healthy, well rested servant ~ even Jesus pulled away from time to time.

I pray this section of prayers empowers you to love and care for yourself as you become who God has destined you to be.

I See You

Praying for the ones who were in a crisis before Corona. You were already in the middle of grieving, in the middle of a divorce, in the middle of not being able to make your ends meet. You were already dealing with feeling "less than" or unmet expectations…and now this. You are putting up a brave front so that people won't know and won't judge you. But you are crumbling on the inside. I really want you to talk to somebody. You've been solving the world's problems and sweeping yours under the rug. You want to be happy and you need to be HEARD. Security and success are important but I want you to also value your SANITY. Piling one crisis on top of another can be devastating. I pray that God will give you the courage to open your heart, the strength to share your pain and the determination to walk in wholeness. It's time. I see you.

I am praying for you.

Be Present

Some of you have been feeling like you've been living in a fog. This past week you had glimpses of feeling like your normal self. Today I pray that you will lean into those feelings. Do something today that reminds you of YOU. Not just the YOU before the pandemic ~ but the YOU before you were hurt, the YOU before you were misunderstood, the YOU before you realized you didn't fit in. That's the YOU the world needs. Stop being anxious about your ultimate purpose. Stop agonizing over what didn't work. Today, take some time to just be present for you. Show up for you and do something that feeds your soul and makes your heart smile. You deserve it. What can you do today that is unquestionably, undoubtedly, irrefutably YOU?

My answer: Today I will go on YouTube and learn a dance/routine. I haven't done that in YEARS and I smiled when it dropped in my spirit. I'll let you know how it goes.

Love y'all for real.

Do Something Today That Relaxes You

Do something today that relaxes you. You carry your world on your shoulders every day. You carry other people in your mind every day. You carry past hurt in your spirit every day. Right now ~ close your eyes ~ see yourself putting everything down and just carrying you. Take that kind of deep breath that you take when get in the car and you are finally able to take off your mask. Breathe. Relax. If you are reading this and thinking "I don't have time for me" you are in the 'at risk' category. You MUST do this. All of those things that you are holding together will fall apart because YOU will eventually fall apart. I pray that today God will help you to calm your spirit. I pray that today you will allow God to fill you with peace. I pray that today you will pause and give God space to restore your soul.

Breathe.

Relax.

I love you and I want you at your best.

I'm praying for you.

Move You to the Top of the List

You do so much to take care of others, so today, I pray that you intentionally do something to take care of you. Move YOU up on your To-Do list. I pray you can move a little bit slower today. I pray you will breathe a little bit deeper today. I pray you will smile longer and laugh harder today. I pray you can free your mind from the worries of the future and be present in the now. God loves you so much. Just sit with that for a moment. God loves you and God desires that you take care of you. You are God's workmanship. You are fearfully and wonderfully made. Today I pray you will take care of you ~ mind, body and spirit. This is my prayer for you ~ and now I pray that you will speak this prayer over yourself as affirmations.

[Read Aloud] *Today, I will move ME up on my To-Do list. Today, I will move slower, breathe deeper, smile longer and laugh harder. I will free my mind from the worries of the future. I will be present in the now. God loves me so much. (Smile and say it again) God loves me so much. I am God's workmanship. I am fearfully and wonderfully made. Today I will take care of me ~ mind, body, and spirit.*

It is so!

Do Something Today That Calms Your Spirit

Do something today that calms your spirit. The conditions of the world have had us anxious and on edge for months and we have accepted an unhealthy amount of anxiety as normal. I pray that, today, you will take the time to be still, be present, and be at peace. I pray that you can tap into the place where there is nothing missing and nothing broken. I pray that you will experience moments where you catch yourself smiling for no reason. I pray that you will have the courage to remove yourself from toxic conversations and ~ if only for today ~ learn to allow people to be negative in your absence and not in your presence. I pray that with every deep breath you take you can:

Inhale peace and exhale chaos.

Inhale power and exhale confusion.

Inhale your purpose and exhale any contradictions.

Be Still. Be present. Be at peace.

I'm praying for you.

Today's Affirmation

I know somehow ~ I know some way; I'm gonna make it. No matter what the test ~ Whatever comes my way, I'm gonna make it. With Jesus on my side, things will work out fine. I'm gonna make it. Thank you, Jesus, for being by my side. Thank you, Jesus, for never leaving me. Thank you, Jesus, for working things out for my good. When things get rough, remind me of this affirmation and help me to trust You more. Help me to move beyond what I feel and to believe what You said. I speak healing and hope. I speak peace and power. It is so ~ in the matchless name of Jesus.

Amen.

I Believe

[Read Aloud] *Today, I choose to trust God in every situation. Today, I will increase my faith on purpose. I will read, say, and do the things that build my faith. As I increase my faith ~ I decrease my fear.*

Today, I will push the enemy out of my thoughts with God's word. I believe that God still has plans for me. I believe that God will still give me the desires of my heart. I believe that God is still working on my behalf ~ even when it doesn't feel like it.

I believe that all of these hurtful and painful things will work together for my good. I believe in God's love. I believe in God's peace. I believe in God's victory. I believe in God.

**Your faith is increased by HEARING. If you didn't read it out loud, do it again. This may be your only self-care moment for today. Don't cheat your spirit. Tap into your faith and shift your day.

I love y'all for real.

Remember Who You Are

Sometimes we take hits in life that cause us to stray away from who we are at our core. We don't always know when it is happening, but sometimes after a toxic relationship, a demeaning job, or even a string of what we think are defeats ~ we look at our life and feel as if we have lost ourselves. I pray that the hits of life will not beat you down to the point where you forget that you are fearfully and wonderfully made. I pray that you will recover your self-esteem, reclaim your self-worth, and find your way back to YOU.

The version of you that is creative and kind.

The version of you that respects yourself and doesn't need the approval of others to shine.

The version of you that unapologetically stands in your own greatness.

God's greatness is a part of your core and cannot be denied. You are a child of the King ~ a descendant of royalty. Remember who you are.

I'm praying for you.

Peace Belongs To Me

Pay attention today to the things and people that make you anxious. Pay attention to what your body does when your anxiety is rising. You know what it feels like when you are getting nervous ~ you need to know what it feels like when you are getting anxious. You cannot conquer or manage anything that you ignore. Here is a quick affirmation for you to read aloud to set your intentions for today. I'm praying today that God's peace will chase you and overtake you. Love y'all!

[Read Aloud]

Peace belongs to me.
Peace is my default.
Peace is my normal.
I know what makes me anxious and I know what calms my spirit.

Today I will manage my anxiety by doing more of what calms me. I speak the peace of God over my day. I speak that I will enjoy divine appointments today that will make me smile and remind me to BREATHE. Today I will take my thoughts captive and I speak peace over confusion, joy over sadness and faith over fear. I open my heart and my mind to things that are true, honest, pure, and lovely. God desires that I have peace. Peace belongs to me. Peace is my default. Peace is my normal. It is so.

Inner Peace

Today I pray that God will give you inner peace. Not just moments of quietness, but moments where God soothes your soul. Moments that are so peaceful and soul-soothing that you can hear God's voice above a whisper. I pray you hear God clearly and make decisions today based on God's answers and not your own anxiety. I know God loves you. I know God cares about what concerns you. I pray that something will happen today that allows you to know it too. I'm praying for you.

Take a deep breath and whisper each sentence during your exhale.
Inhale. Exhale: *I am loved.*
Inhale. Exhale: *I am at peace.*
Inhale. Exhale: *God hears my prayers.*
Inhale. Exhale: *God will answer.*

Just Breathe

Thanking God for the makings of a beautiful day! I pray that YOU will have a moment to pause the business and the busyness of life to enjoy moments of self-care. I'm asking God to help YOU to calm your spirit and allow you to bask in God's unconditional, unchanging and unfailing love. I decree and declare according to God's word that today YOU will experience unspeakable joy, unmerited favor and a peace that surpasses your own understanding.

I speak a sacred space for you to just BREATHE today. Breathe in peace and exhale chaos. Breathe in clarity and exhale confusion. Today, my friend, I speak that you will breathe in the divine rhythm of grace and mercy. Inhale. Exhale. Nothing missing. Nothing broken.

I'm praying for you.

Mindset Is Everything

Mindset is everything. There is so much power to move forward or stay stagnant in your thoughts. Today I pray for the ones who are having a hard time overcoming anxiety. I pray that you can align your thoughts with the Word and the Will of God during your anxious moments. Take a deep breath.

Be still and know:
God cares about you.
God is FOR you.
God is with you.
God is guarding you.
God is working on your behalf.
I love you and I'm praying for you.

TIP: Change the 'you' to 'me' in the God statements above to make them affirmations. Whisper them until you feel calm again.

Praying For A Pause

Praying for a PAUSE for the DOERS today. The ones who are always DOING for others and sometimes forget to DO for themselves. I pray that you are kind to yourself today. I pray that when you sit still you don't feel guilty because of all the things you 'could be doing'. I pray that with every deep breath you take God would relax your mind and restore your soul.

**Take a deep breath. Inhale 3-2-1 ~~ Exhale 3-2-1

You are ALWAYS thinking.

**Take a deep breath. Inhale 3-2-1 ~~ Exhale 3-2-1

I'm not asking for God to change that about you ~ I'm just praying that God helps you change what you are thinking about.

**Take a deep breath. Inhale 3-2-1 ~~ Exhale 3-2-1

God loves you. God desires that you have peace. God desires that you have a well-rested mind and body. If Jesus had to pull away from time to time...so do you.

**Take a deep breath. Inhale 3-2-1 ~~ Exhale 3-2-1

Now SMILE...

You're doing your best.

It's going to all come together.

God is working on your behalf.

Relax and be restored.

I love you and I'm praying for you.

Center Your Thoughts

Here are few affirmations to help center your thoughts today:
Today I will embrace the greatness within me.
Today I will accept responsibility for my own happiness and development.
Today I will continue to build a circle that encourages and inspires me.
Today I will inhale confidence and exhale doubt.
I have the power to create change and I will start with me.
~Love y'all!

Healing Scriptures

I believe in praying God's Word over every situation, especially when praying for healing. These are some of the Scriptures I speak and pray over those who are dealing with illness. This section includes Scriptures that speak directly to healing and other Scriptures that encourage and lift the spirits of the sick. There are many others, so please continue to study and add to this list as you expand your time in prayer.

Psalm 103:2-4 (NIV)

²Praise the Lord, my soul,
and forget not all his benefits—
³who forgives all your sins
and heals all your diseases,
⁴who redeems your life from the pit
and crowns you with love and compassion,

Psalm 41:3 (ESV)

³The Lord sustains him on his sickbed;
in his illness you restore him to full health

James 5:15-16 (NIV)

¹⁵And the prayer offered in faith will make the sick person well; the Lord will raise them up. If they have sinned, they will be forgiven. ¹⁶Therefore confess your sins to each other and pray for each other so that you may be healed. The prayer of a righteous person is powerful and effective.

3 John 2:2 (NRSV)

Beloved, I pray that all may go well with you and that you may
be in good health, just as it is well with your soul.

Jeremiah 30:17a (NIV)

But I will restore you to health
and heal your wounds,'
declares the Lord,

Matthew 10:1 (NIV)

Jesus called his twelve disciples to him and gave them authority to drive out impure spirits and to heal every disease and sickness.

Philippians 4:19 (NRSV)

And my God will fully satisfy every need of yours according to his riches in glory in Christ Jesus.

Psalm 6:2 (NKJV)

Have mercy on me, O Lord, for I *am* weak;
O Lord, heal me, for my bones are troubled.

Proverbs 3:5-8 (NIV)

⁵Trust in the Lord with all your heart
and lean not on your own understanding;
⁶in all your ways submit to him,
and he will make your paths straight.
⁷Do not be wise in your own eyes;
fear the Lord and shun evil.
⁸This will bring health to your body
and nourishment to your bones.

Philippians 4:6-7 (NIV)

⁶Do not be anxious about anything, but in every situation, by prayer and petition, with thanksgiving, present your requests to God.
⁷And the peace of God, which transcends all understanding, will guard your hearts and your minds in Christ Jesus.

Psalm 107:19-22 (NIV)

[19]Then they cried to the Lord in their trouble,
and he saved them from their distress.
[20]He sent out his word and healed them;
he rescued them from the grave.
[21]Let them give thanks to the Lord for his unfailing love
and his wonderful deeds for mankind.
[22]Let them sacrifice thank offerings
and tell of his works with songs of joy.

2 Chronicles 7:14 (NIV)

if My people who are called by My name
will humble themselves,
and pray and seek My face,
and turn from their wicked ways,
then I will hear from heaven,
and will forgive their sin and heal their land.

Luke 10:9 (NIV)

Heal the sick who are there and tell them,
'The kingdom of God has come near to you.'

Isaiah 57:18-19 (NIV)

[18]I have seen their ways, but I will heal them;
I will guide them and restore comfort to Israel's mourners,
[19]creating praise on their lips.
Peace, peace, to those far and near,"
says the Lord. "And I will heal them."

Exodus 23:25-26 (NRSV)
²⁵You shall worship the Lord your God,
and I will bless your bread and your water;
and I will take sickness away from among you.
²⁶No one shall miscarry or be barren in your land;
I will fulfill the number of your days.

Psalm 118:16-17 (NIV)
¹⁶The Lord's right hand is lifted high;
the Lord's right hand has done mighty things!"
¹⁷I will not die but live,
and will proclaim what the Lord has done.

Isaiah 41:10 (NRSV)
do not fear, for I am with you,
do not be afraid, for I am your God;
I will strengthen you; I will help you,
I will uphold you with my victorious right hand.

Jeremiah 1:12 (NRSV)
Then the Lord said to me,
"You have seen well, for I am watching over
my word to perform it."

Hebrews 13:8 (NRSV)
Jesus Christ is the same yesterday and today and forever.

Nahum 1:9 (NKJV)
What do you conspire against the Lord?
He will make an utter end *of it*.
Affliction will not rise up a second time.

2 Corinthians 10:3-5 (NKJV)

³For though we walk in the flesh, we do not war according to the flesh. ⁴For the weapons of our warfare *are* not carnal but mighty in God for pulling down strongholds, ⁵casting down arguments and every high thing that exalts itself against the knowledge of God, bringing every thought into captivity to the obedience of Christ,

Hebrews 10:23 (NKJV)

Let us hold fast the confession of *our* hope without wavering, for He who promised *is* faithful.

(NIV)

Let us hold unswervingly to the confession of *our* hope, for He who promised *is* faithful.

Hebrews 10:35-37 (NIV)

³⁵So do not throw away your confidence; it will be richly rewarded. ³⁶You need to persevere so that when you have done the will of God, you will receive what he has promised. ³⁷For "In just a little while, he who is coming will come and will not delay."

(NKJV)

³⁵Do not, therefore, abandon that confidence of yours; it brings a great reward. ³⁶For you need endurance, so that when you have done the will of God, you may receive what was promised. ³⁷For yet "in a very little while, the one who is coming will come and will not delay;

I Peter 2:24 (NRSV)

He himself bore our sins in his body on the cross, so that, free from sins, we might live for righteousness; by his wounds you have been healed.

Psalm 30 (NLT)

¹I will exalt you, Lord, for you rescued me.
You refused to let my enemies triumph over me.
²O Lord my God, I cried to you for help,
and you restored my health.
³You brought me up from the grave, O Lord.
You kept me from falling into the pit of death.
⁴Sing to the Lord, all you godly ones!
Praise his holy name.
⁵For his anger lasts only a moment,
but his favor lasts a lifetime!
Weeping may last through the night,
but joy comes with the morning.
⁶When I was prosperous, I said,
"Nothing can stop me now!"
⁷Your favor, O Lord, made me as secure as a mountain.
Then you turned away from me, and I was shattered.
⁸I cried out to you, O Lord.
I begged the Lord for mercy, saying,
⁹"What will you gain if I die,
if I sink into the grave?
Can my dust praise you?
Can it tell of your faithfulness?
¹⁰Hear me, Lord, and have mercy on me.
Help me, O Lord."
¹¹You have turned my mourning into joyful dancing.
You have taken away my clothes of mourning and clothed me with joy,
¹²that I might sing praises to you and not be silent.
O Lord my God, I will give you thanks forever!

Psalm 33 20-22 (NIV)
²⁰We wait in hope for the Lord;
he is our help and our shield.
²¹In him our hearts rejoice,
for we trust in his holy name.
²²May your unfailing love be with us, Lord,
even as we put our hope in you.

Psalm 130 (NIV)
A song of ascents.
¹Out of the depths I cry to you, Lord;
²Lord, hear my voice.
Let your ears be attentive
to my cry for mercy.
³If you, Lord, kept a record of sins,
Lord, who could stand?
⁴But with you there is forgiveness,
so that we can, with reverence, serve you.
⁵I wait for the Lord, my whole being waits,
and in his word I put my hope.
⁶I wait for the Lord
more than watchmen wait for the morning,
more than watchmen wait for the morning.
⁷Israel, put your hope in the Lord,
for with the Lord is unfailing love
and with him is full redemption.
⁸He himself will redeem Israel
from all their sins.

Psalm 46:10 (NKJV)
Be still, and know that I *am* God;

Names of God

God is called by many names—Jehovah, Elohim, Adonai—and those names are precious because they describe who God is and what God has promised to God's people. There are names that God calls God's self and names that people have attributed to God. I have included a list, albeit not exhaustive, that will encourage your hearts as you seek God in prayer.

Hebrew Names of God

Adonai
[ah-daw-nahy]
"Lord" (Genesis 15:2; Judges 6:15)

Elohim
[el-oh-heem]
God "Creator, Mighty and Strong"
(Genesis 17:7; Jeremiah 31:33)

El Shaddai
[el-shah-dahy]
"God Almighty, The Mighty One of Jacob"
(Genesis 49:24; Psalm 132:2,5)

El Elyon
[el-el-yohn]
"Most High" (Deuteronomy 26:19)

Hebrew Names of God

El Roi
[el-roh-ee]
"God who Sees" (Genesis 16:13)

El Olam
[el-oh-lahm]
"Everlasting God" (Psalm 90:1-3)

El Gibhor
[el-ghee-bohr]
"Mighty God" (Isaiah 9:6)

Yhwh / Yahweh
[yah-way]

Jehovah
[ji-hoh-veh]
"LORD" (Deuteronomy 6:4; Daniel 9:14)

Jehovah Jireh
[ji-hoh-veh -ji-reh]
"The Lord Will Provide" (Genesis 22:14)

Jehovah Rophe or Jehovah Rapha
[ji-hoh-veh -raw-faw]
"The Lord Who Heals" (Exodus 15:26)

Jehovah Nissi
[ji-hoh-veh -nee-see]
"The Lord Our Banner" (Exodus 17:15)

Jehovah M'kaddesh or Jehovah Maccaddeshcem
[ji-hoh-veh -meh-kad-esh]
"The Lord Who Sanctifies, Makes Holy"
(Leviticus 20:8; Ezekiel 37:28)

Jehovah Shalom
[ji-hoh-veh -shah-lohm]
"The Lord Our Peace" (Judges 6:24)

Jehovah Elohim
[ji-hoh-veh -el-oh-him]
"LORD God" (Genesis 2:4; Psalm 59:5)

Jehovah Tsidkenu
[ji-hoh-veh -tzid-kay-noo]
"The Lord Our Righteousness" (Jeremiah 33:16)

Jehovah Rohi
[ji-hoh-veh -roh-hee]
"The Lord Our Shepherd" (Psalm 23:1)

Jehovah Shammah
[ji-hoh-veh -sham-mahw]
"The Lord Is There" (Ezekiel 48:35)

Jehovah Sabaoth
[ji-hoh-veh -sah-bah-ohth]
"The Lord of Hosts" (Isaiah 1:24; Psalm 46:7)

Other Names Ascribed To God Throughout Scripture

Abba Father

All Consuming Fire

Alpha and Omega

Ancient of Days

Architect

Builder

Creator

Creator of Heaven and Earth

Dwelling Place

Eternal King

Everlasting Light

Father

Father of Compassion

Fortress

God of Abraham, Isaac, and Jacob

God of All Comfort

God of All Grace

God Our Father

Heavenly Father

Helper Hiding Place

High Tower

Holy One

Holy One of Israel

I am that I am

Judge

Just and Mighty One

Keeper

Other Names Ascribed To God Throughout Scripture

King of Glory
King of kings
Lifter Up of My Head
Lord of lords
Maker of Heaven and Earth
My Glory
My Song
My Strength
Potter
Refuge
Righteous One
Rock
Rock of Ages
Rock of Israel
Ruler of All Things
Shade
Shelter
Shepherd
Shield
Sovereign
Sovereign Lord
Strong Tower
Stronghold of My Life
Sustainer of my Soul
The First and the Last
True and Living God
Who is and who was and who is to come

Dr. Karren D. Todd

Dr. Karren D. Todd is a dynamic speaker, powerful motivator, author and certified professional coach. After serving 15 years in full-time ministry, with eight years as Senior Associate Pastor, Karren shifted to serving God as the Executive Director of POWER Ministries, Inc and CEO of Empowerment Coaching and Consulting. Karren supports clients in ministry and in the marketplace through individual and group coaching, workshops, pastoral counseling and church consulting.

Karren serves on the Board of Directors for Leadership Memphis and the Memphis Urban League Guild. She has received many honors including TSD's Women of Excellence, Female Pastor of the Year and the 2019 Dress for Success Entrepreneurial Spirit Award. Karren is a published author with 2 of her books landing on Amazon and Kindle's Best-Selling lists. She serves as a Clergy Coach for the Clergy Coaching Network and hosts a weekly radio show called *SOAR with Coach Karren*.

Karren is currently serving her denomination as the Minister of New Church Formation and recently began a Chaplain Residency with a local hospital in Memphis TN.

Karren holds a Master of Divinity degree from Memphis Theological Seminary and received her Doctor of Ministry degree in Pastoral Counseling in May 2020.

For more information about Dr. Todd's
- ~ Workshops
- ~ Books
- ~ Seminars and Presentations
- ~ Individual Consultations

visit **www.karrentodd.com**

Made in the USA
Columbia, SC
08 June 2021